Deal!

Guidelines for a Flawless Negotiation

The 6 P's of Negotiation and the
Methodology that Ensures
Robust Negotiations

Negotiating with a Vision + Selling with Passion =
Deal!

Deal!

by
Dr. Habib Chamoun - Nicolás

With the special collaboration of
Lic. Marcela Farah Guerra
and
Pablo M. Linzoain, MBA, MSc.

Negotiating with a Vision + Selling with Passion = Deal!

**KN
Keynegotiations**

Copyright©2004-2014 by Dr. Habib Chamoun-Nicolás

Library of Congress Control Number: 2004091700

First Edition, Spanish. February 2003, Kingwood, Texas
Second Edition, Spanish. July 2003, Kingwood, Texas
Third Edition, English. March 2004, Kingwood, Texas

Cover and interior pages design:
    Lic. Enriqueta González Rodríguez
Translation:
    Leonor McCall-Rodriguez
Text:
    D.R. © 2004-2014, Dr. Habib Chamoun- Nicolás

This Edition:
Published by Keynegotiations
D.R.© 2004-2014, Dr. Habib Chamoun-Nicolás
Keynegotiations
P.O. Box 6558
Kingwood, Texas 77325
ISBN: 978-0-9728317-2-7

All rights reserved. Beyond the legal rights related to the research, private study, commentary or reviews, this publication or any portion of the content in Spanish or any other language may not be directly or indirectly copied, registered, published, reproduced, modified, performed, displayed, sold, transmitted, published, broadcast, rewritten for broadcast or publication or redistributed in any form or medium including but not limited to systems of information recovery, mechanical, photochemical, electronic, magnetic, electro-optical, photocopy or any other medium invented or to be invented, without the prior specific permission in writing from the author.

Commentary on *Deal – Guidelines for a Flawless Negotiation by Dr. Habib Chamoun-Nicolas*

Deal is a book that has many wonderful characteristics. It makes the reader join the author, Dr. Habib Chamoun-Nicolás, in a vision about negotiations that runs counter to that offered by the popular press. The press almost always focuses on price as the principal objective of negotiation. Meanwhile, Dr. Chamoun holds other points as important in preparing the context in which the good salesman serves (instead of services) the client. When the salesman broaches subjects in what seem non-essential topics of conversation, at least in regard to the price of the product or service under consideration, the conversation turns to topics that make it easier for the salesman to serve the client, not only on this occasion, but on many others that grow in a long string of consultations, purchases, and referrals to other new clients. What the beginner to these topics notices moreover, is the genuine preoccupation of the salesman to explore the client's real needs, taking the salesman to untold horizons of service and of success.

Dr. Chamoun-Nicolás has dealt with these topics all over the world. He is not only fluent in his examination of the relations between and among Mexicans and other Latin Americans, but also displays an acute sense of observation that is on target for others as well. His extensive experience in the area of negotiation has taken Dr. Chamoun-Nicolás to distant corners of the earth, although in each of these there is a genuine need for a good negotiation and a positive result. This book brings together those observations, which I have seen him offer to Beijing China airport managers, as well as to Mexican businessmen in Houston. I have seen him negotiate with Middle Easterners and Europeans in the oil business.

I consider Dr. Habib Chamoun-Nicolás a true gentleman, who may one day lecture at Monterrey Tech, or at Thunderbird Graduate School of International Business, and on another, offer a presentation at a hotel in Jamaica, or Ecuador, or any European country. But more than a gentleman, he is a super negotiator, whose education harks back to Texas and Mexico, and whose pearls of wisdom are at your fingertips in this marvelous book.

Rodolfo J. Cortina, Ph.D.
Professor[1] & Director of the Center for the Americas
Vice President for Undergraduate Studies, University of Houston
Vice Chancellor for International Affairs, University of Houston System

[1] Retired.

Contents

Acknowledgments	10
Prologue	11
Introduction	13
I. A New Trend in the School of Sales	**15**
I.1 The Virtuous Circle and Synergy of Negotiation	19
I.2 CHAMOUN Methodology of Business Development	25
I.3 Robust Negotiations	27
I.4 Long Term Client Relationships	29
II. The 6 P's of Robust Negotiation	**33**
II.1 The Dimensions of Negotiation	37
II.2 The 6 P's of Negotiation	39
i **Person**	43
ii **Product**	46
iii **Problem**	49
iv **Process**	51
v **Power**	55
vi **Prognosis**	57
III. The Culture and 6 P's of Robust Negotiation	**61**
III.1 Culture and International Negotiation	65
III.2 The Culture and 6 P's	71
III.3 Global Vision of Negotiation	73
III.4 The Great Differences Between Cultures as the Driving Event of Negotiation. Without Differences, There is No Need to Negotiate	74
III.5 Strategy and Behaviors in International Negotiations	86
IV. Case Studies and Experiences of Negotiation	**89**
IV.1 Chronicles of a Failed Negotiation	93
IV.2 A Negotiation that Exceeded Expectations	96
IV.3 A Negotiation is a Continuous Dance of Interests Behind Positions	99

IV.4 When the Big Ones Lose Power	103
IV.5 The Difference is in "The Closing Moment"	106
IV.6 Negotiating in Difficult Situations	112
IV.7 The Imbalance of Power and Win/Win Negotiations	117
IV.8 The Invisible Barriers of Negotiation	119
IV.9 Establishing the Standards of a Good Negotiation	123
IV.10 The Key is Preparing the Negotiation	127
IV.11 Negotiating with Difficult People	128
IV.12 Negotiation of a Perishable Product Past its Expiration Date	130

V. Efficient Techniques for Successful Negotiating 137

V.1 The 14 Factors that Influence Successful Negotiations	141
V.2 The 14 Efficient Techniques for Negotiating Large Projects	143
V.3 How Do You Gain Power in High-Profitability Projects?	153
V.4 Power and International Negotiations	162

Appendix

A.1 How to Achieve Robust Negotiations with Latin Americans.	167
A.2 The Argentinean Style of Negotiation by Pablo M. Linzoain	188

Bibliography	217
Commentary	233
About the Author	224
What People Are Saying About the Author	225
About the Collaborator	227
Get Ready to Deal	229

Vae Victis…(Woe to the Vanquished)

In memory of my brother Anuar,
who rests in my heart and thoughts,
from whom I learned that to negotiate
efficiently, you must be yourself.

Acknowledgments

To God, for giving me the light to go on in moments of chaos.

To my wife, Marcela, my "Great Woman" and our children, Habib, Emile, Antoine and Marcelle, for their patience, love and blessings.

To my mother, "La Nena Nicolás", whom I will always admire for her ideals, my father, Habib, for his teachings, and my siblings, Soraya and Yamal for sharing my dreams.

To Pablo M. Linzoain, experienced international negotiator, for his valuable contribution to the second edition of "Deal", on the subject of international negotiations and culture.

To Bob Junke, for allowing us to mention the concepts of the Adventace methodology as of the second edition of "Deal"; as to Barbara Hauser for her commentary and contribution to this theme.

To Leonor McCall Rodriguez from the Latino Speakers Bureau for her great job translating this book.

To my friends, Dr. Randy Hazlett and Don Dixon for reviewing the contents of the book to assure its quality.

To Mrs. Derry Summer for her kind efforts of proof reading "Deal".

To all of you, who have participated in my courses and consulting, clients, colleagues, teachers, friends and to you, who are about to read this book, "Deal".

Prologue

Negotiations are intrinsic to human nature and to our everyday life. At work, we negotiate with our peers, supervisors and coworkers to effectively achieve the goals of our organization. We do the same with our spouses in order to satisfy our expectations and the desires to build a positive and happy life together. With our children, we negotiate as part of the process of their upbringing. We even negotiate with ourselves when, for example, we are reconciling eating something for which we have an intense craving (like a food high in calories, fat and cholesterol, but very "appetizing"), with the objectives of health and/or aesthetics so important in our quality of life. To negotiate is definitely inherent to human nature.

"Deal" speaks to all of us and helps us to better handle the large quantity of roles we play and the responsibilities that we carry out. *"Deal"* helps us understand and learn about the negotiation process and become more intelligent and skillful at it.

Dr. Habib Chamoun educates, entertains and intellectually seduces us with his work and his writing style. As an introduction, he takes us, through the description of a new business environment he calls "A New Trend in the School of Sales", to see negotiation in a broader perspective that includes the context, the participating actors and the subject being negotiated.

Subsequently, he offers a clear, practical and effective methodology that enables us to negotiate in a "robust" manner. While reading this book, it is easily inferred that Habib is an experienced negotiator and scholar, who deliberately incorporates at every turn, the human side and the importance of a negotiation based on dignity and personal values in both national and international scenarios.

In chapter IV, "Case Studies and Experiences of Negotiation", we see the use of this methodology in a smooth flow of examples of cases and situations where it might be put into practice. The presentation of specific and practical situations, the analysis of the same through the proposed methodology and the conclusions to which the reader is drawn, are simply an intellectual delight that allows us to manage the process of negotiation skillfully and intelligently.

"Deal" is an excellent work by Habib that not only helps us negotiate better, but also enables us to become better individuals. Its concepts, ideas and methodology allow us to think strategically, build better judgments, make better decisions, and design positive courses of action. *"Deal"* is easy in its language, practical in its applications, structured in its methodology and interesting in its reading. *"Deal"* helps us learn and at the same time, enjoy the learning process.

Negotiating, under Habib's perspective, means searching for the understanding of people, their values and the dynamics of their interactions (negotiations) at work, at home, at school, in self-reflection and across all the vectors of the human process. *"Deal"* has negotiation as a topic, but its essence lies within people and their values.

Dr. Jaime Alonso Gómez Aguirre
Professor of Strategy and International Business
Dean[2] of the Graduate School of Business
Administration and Leadership
Monterrey Tec, (EGADE-ITESM)

[2] Former Dean.

Introduction

It has been proven that selling without planning limits the power of negotiation. In his book, "Business Development" 3rd edition, Dr. Habib Chamoun- Nicolás, presents different helpful tools that allow salesmen to arrive prepared for the negotiation.

The main focus of this book, **Deal**, is on the domain of negotiation, and it provides the guidelines to succeed in any business negotiation

Here, we introduce the concepts of the virtuous circle and the synergy of the negotiation and the CHAMOUN Methodology of Business Development ©2003. We integrate the CHAMOUN Methodology of Sales©2003 (the 10 P's of Sales) that we presented in the book "Business Development", with the 6P's of Negotiation that are introduced in this book. Furthermore, we describe how the factor of culture plays a role or influences the 6P's of Negotiation.

With the purpose of relating the concepts we present with actual cases, we narrate some realistic situations where the names are fictitious. Any resemblance to the reality of some readers is a mere coincidence.

The purpose of **Deal** is that the reader obtains a global vision of the domain of negotiation, and as a result, increases the strategic panoramas that can be used in different business scenarios. **Deal** is a guide whose objective is to encourage the reader to follow step-by-step the sequence presented, applicable to any situation and be able to avoid the most common flaws of a negotiation. "Practice makes perfect", and I invite you to practice the concepts and ideas I present in the following chapters and will be happy to receive your real life examples of successes and / or failures. Many of the ideas that came together in the writing of **Deal** have been the result of observations that I have collected from thousands of people from Mexico, Latin America and the United States. After reading **Deal** if you want to obtain insights on how to make Great Deals with Latin Americans please be sure to review the appendix material, were I have included some of my own research on the subject.

Enjoy it.

Habib Chamoun-Nicolás

"Ideas are a capital that bears interest
only in the hands of talent." - Rivarol

Chapter 1

One day, while standing in line to go through security for my flight to Mexico at Houston George Bush International Airport, I suddenly heard a voice shouting, "Does anyone speak French?" I raised my hand, and the blonde stewardess said, "Great, Sir. I really appreciate your help. I am having a communication problem with this elderly Frenchman. He insists on bringing his knife to peel apples on board the plane, and as you know with security issues, there's no way we can allow this. Could you please explain the situation to him, for he doesn't speak English?" On this simple, ordinary day, I had an impromptu opportunity to negotiate between two very different cultures. I did have a vested interest in the outcome, however, as I wanted my flight to be safe and on time, and this man was holding up the line. As I engaged the elderly gentleman in conversation, he replied, "I don't understand the problem with bringing my grandfather's knife on board. I am attached to this knife. It is a souvenir from the past." I told the Frenchman that because of security reasons he could not carry that knife onto the plane. Following a 4 minute conversation, the man appealed, "Okay, can you include it with my luggage?" The airline employee said, "It is too late. His luggage is already checked in." I responded, "What are his options?" She said, "Well, he can either surrender the knife, or he can trust me to mail it. Do you know how much it costs to mail something to France?" I answered, "I don't know — maybe $10 maximum." I informed the man that it was too late to include it in checked luggage and that his options were to leave it or mail it. I told him that he needed to trust the employee, and the mailing cost would be around $10. He pleasantly agreed to leave the knife and have it mailed. Even with such a short conversation, a hostile situation gave way to rapport and trust. Regardless of the culture, there are ways to solve problems and achieve results such that everybody wins.

15

In every moment of daily life, negotiation takes a prominent place. The better we handle small deals, the better we will become at negotiating complex deals. We have to understand both parties and what they want. The airline employee needed to follow the rules, and the French traveler needed to keep his grandfather's knife. The parties were at an impasse because of cultural barriers. They didn't understand one another's language enough to communicate their concerns effectively and negotiate a deal. Negotiation is a matter of understanding the 6 P's: the **People**, the **Process**, the **Products** being negotiated, the **Problem**, the **Prognosis** for success, and the sources of **Power** in negotiating.

Throughout this book you will find tools to dissect a negotiation into understandable parts, helping you become a more skillful negotiator.

The New Trend in the School of Sales

"A global vision of negotiation is the key to success. In contrast, shortsightedness on the part of the negotiator focused only on price, is generally the source of failure."
Dr. Habib Chamoun-Nicolás

This chapter contains the following topics:

    I.1 The Virtuous Circle and Synergy of Negotiation

    I.2 CHAMOUN Methodology of Business Development

    I.3 Robust Negotiations

    I.4 Long Term Client Relationships

I.1 The Virtuous Circle and Synergy of Negotiation

The new school of sales forces the traditional salesman to convert into a Business Developer for his client, as is shown in "The Virtuous Circle and Synergy of Negotiation" in Diagrams I.1 and I.2. The global vision begins by focusing on the need of the client and the Business Development of our client. If, for a moment, we think, "How do we develop our client's business? What can we offer him to make his business grow?" This leads us to promote robust and efficient negotiations. As a general rule, robust negotiations can be completed in three or less visits to the client, and are conducted in such a way that the client will call us again. Thus, we repeat the new business development circle. Robust negotiations lead us to develop relationships with our clients that are progressively stronger and longer term and require more of our attention, similar to a tree that grows and flourishes when well cared for. The same effect occurs with clients. The more robust our relationship is with them, the more it will require constant cultivation. The relationship grows from a robust negotiation with the client, and as a result, so does the development of new business.

Today, the salesman requires more preparation, knowledge and tools that will aid the process of closing the Deal.

Back in the 70's, the salesman only needed to work industriously, knocking on doors, and the client would buy from him. The concepts of "client service", "added value", "quality in service" and "global competition" were unnecessary and nonexistent. The salesman only needed to be sure to have the product, and product was all he sold.

In today's world, a global vision of the process of sales and negotiation is required. Amongst other things, the salesman requires support tools to present and propose his services or products, to understand his market, to learn about the needs of his clients, to perceive the strengths and weaknesses of his competition, and to recognize why they need his products and services.

The reality is that today, a successful salesman no longer sells products or services to his clients. He sells solutions for specific needs.

This implies that the salesman must know about not only the needs of his client, but also know about the clients of his client and the whole value chain (formed by the vendors, processes, etc.). For example, if we look at the case of the salesman of maintenance products, before selling the product to the client, he must be sure that it will really be able to satisfy his client's needs by analyzing the impact that his services or products will have on his client's business.

Let's say you are a salesman for a hardware store, where you sell all types of tools or accessories for replacement or improvement in one's home or workplace. Ask yourself for a moment, who needs faucets for their sinks? Who would be your main client? It could be housewives, or plumbers, amongst others. Suppose your client, the housewife, arrives at the hardware store to buy a faucet for her sink because it stopped working. If you try to sell her a faucet without getting detailed information on what her problem is, you may not solve her problem. If on the contrary, you help her understand what the source of her problem is, you may sell her the faucet and perhaps another sink.

In a consulting project, something similar occurs. Often the client does not know what he really needs. The present-day salesman must go beyond selling apparent solutions, and must get to the root of the problem and find out what real need lies hidden behind it.

Current sales have gone from being a simple sale of "products" to a solution for our clients' problems. We've discussed and offered tools for this in the book "Business Development", to help plan a more efficient sale, such as the 10 P's of the Methodology of Sales and tools for carrying out successful presentations and proposals.

In this book, we have mentally divided negotiation into 6 P's. If we analyze many everyday negotiations we conduct, for example, be it an argument between a married couple or the most complex negotiation, such as for a multimillion dollar consulting project, we can visualize breaking down the process of negotiation into 6 P's:

PERSON: This is the P that characterizes whom we are negotiating with. Here we must take into account if the client comes from a culture different from ours, if they possess different values, behaviors, principles, perceptions and aspirations than our own, and if we are dealing with a man or a woman.

PRODUCT: This P characterizes what is being negotiated. This could be the purchase or sale of a home, engineering services, a pen or a spare part, among other things. Products or services are characterized by this P to simplify the process. Here, it is important to note the intrinsic characteristics of the product or service to be sold, and most importantly of all, visualize how these characteristics translate into benefits that satisfy the needs of our clients. We should note that the benefits do not exist unless our clients require them.

PROBLEM: This P characterizes the conflictive negotiation with multiple problems, whether we caused them, the PERSON we are negotiating with is conflictive, or the negotiation is in itself conflictive in nature, as in a divorce, a lawsuit, or an argument.

PROCESS: This P characterizes the very essence of the negotiation. This is something that starts at a point in time and has a determined duration. In this part, it is important to understand that organizations have norms, rules and laws by which they abide, in consequence, a process of negotiation.

POWER: This P characterizes the perception sustained of oneself in the context of the negotiation. This means the power a person or thing has over another when they negotiate really depends most of the time on the perception that one has over the other. Stated in another fashion, the power we have as we negotiate is derived from the perception the counterpart has of us.

PROGNOSIS: This last P is something that is beyond the control of the persons who are negotiating. It's convenient to do our homework to achieve a good idea or knowledge of the Persons, Product, Problem, Process and Power in the negotiation, since the Prognosis may be governed by external forces, i.e., the market. As such, it is necessary to have a clear vision of the environment that surrounds the negotiation.

If we analyze and understand the 6 P's in each negotiation, we will obtain a global vision of the same and will be able to close more efficient deals. By observing the most successful negotiators, we have determined that they all have something in common, a global vision. It is also very common that the negotiator with the shortsighted vision of "price" will fail in the long term. If, on the contrary, you wish to become a successful negotiator, we invite you to follow the steps of **Deal**. By analyzing the 6 P's in the case of a negotiation, we can decide on the best strategy to pursue, as shown later on in Diagram II.2 (Savage, Blair and Sorenson, 1989).

For example, if both the relationship with the person and the product are very important to us, then the negotiation strategy to follow is cooperative "win / win."

If, on the contrary, neither the person nor the product is worth it, we should avoid the negotiation.

In another case, where the relationship with the person is very important, but the product isn't, the most common strategy is to allow the counterpart to carry out the negotiation. Finally, when the product is more important than the relationship with the person, the strategy of the negotiation becomes competitive.

We'll also see how culture affects the 6 P's of negotiation. In different cultures there exist intrinsic factors associated with each culture that will directly affect the negotiation. Since people possess different aspirations, we can't expect everyone to think or act as we do. "Trato hecho" in Spanish, "Fait accomplie" in French and "Deal" in English express the same thing in different languages, the trust gained by the parties that reach a successful agreement. In conclusion, knowing and understanding in depth what "moves" the other culture will give you the ability to close deals more efficiently.

In the final chapters of this book, we mention the most efficient techniques for negotiating any project. Many times, though we find ourselves at the ideal point for closing the deal, we don't succeed, because we don't have the "closing mentality." As a result, we do not detect that for the counterpart it is the "ideal moment" to close. This type of situation, as well as the invisible barriers to negotiation, will be discussed later on. Remember that not all negotiations are "win / win" (cooperative). There are some that exist where one wins and the other doesn't win as much (competitive). We will analyze them both.

Another topic we will cover is that not everything is negotiable. Additionally, there are things that don't need to be negotiated. They are a given and it is just a question of asking for them. Then we must focus our energy on what is truly negotiable.

With this focus we become more effective as we negotiate. We will also discuss how to concede what we don't need to the other party, if it is valuable to him. We will mention some cases of everyday negotiations, with the intention of establishing these concepts, replicating what has been well done and not repeating mistakes.

Business Development

Robust Negotiations

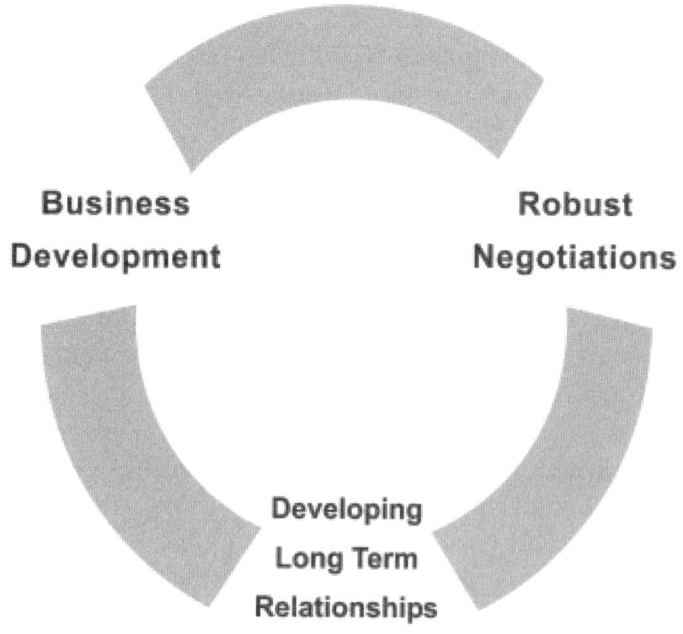

Developing Long Term Relationships

Diagram. I.1 The Virtuous Circle and Synergy of Negotiation

1.2 CHAMOUN Methodology of Business Development

The Methodology of Business Development differs from the Methodology of Sales. The latter allows us to identify the decision makers, assess the opportunity, identify the types of salesmen and determine the client's purpose. The CHAMOUN Methodology of Business Development helps us visualize the "whole picture" and obtain a global vision of the negotiation, the 10 P's of sales (see the book "Business Development"), plus the 6 P's of Negotiation described here. The more methodical we become, the simpler the sale and the closing become. In the case of the sale, we'll analyze it according to

- prospecting,
- presentation,
- proposal to client,
- opportunity to influence the process,
- salesman influence on the process,
- power,
- rejecting bad opportunities,
- using tools for winning presentations and proposals.

All this is encompassed within the virtuous circle and synergy of negotiation in Diagram I.2. In the following diagram (Chart 1.1) we see the 10 P's of the CHAMOUN Methodology of Sales. Remember that the objective of the 10 P's is to minimize the bad opportunities so we can focus specifically on the good ones and be more efficient in taking them to a successful closing. Observing salesmen in the field doing their job has revealed that the successful negotiator has the ability to see the "whole picture".

Prepare yourself	Propose successful strategies
Picture the different customer decision makers and influence entities	Plan actions to make it happen
Position yourself in one of the Chamoun's four types of salesman model, according to your customer (or service provider) relationship	Preview of a tryout exercise with a pioneering test
Proof a profitable return on investment, linking the value added by products and services to the customer needs and wants	Present and Propose to customers successfully (Shipley Associates Proposal Guide, 2001)
Put down on paper extensive list of strengths and weaknesses	Predict and Proclaim success.

Chart I.1 The 10 P's of the CHAMOUN Methodology of Sales from the book "Business Development"

After reviewing the 10 P's of sales, we must understand how the 6 P's of Negotiation fit in this context, as will be shown later in Diagram III.2. We call this joint concept of sales and negotiations: the CHAMOUN Methodology of Business Development.

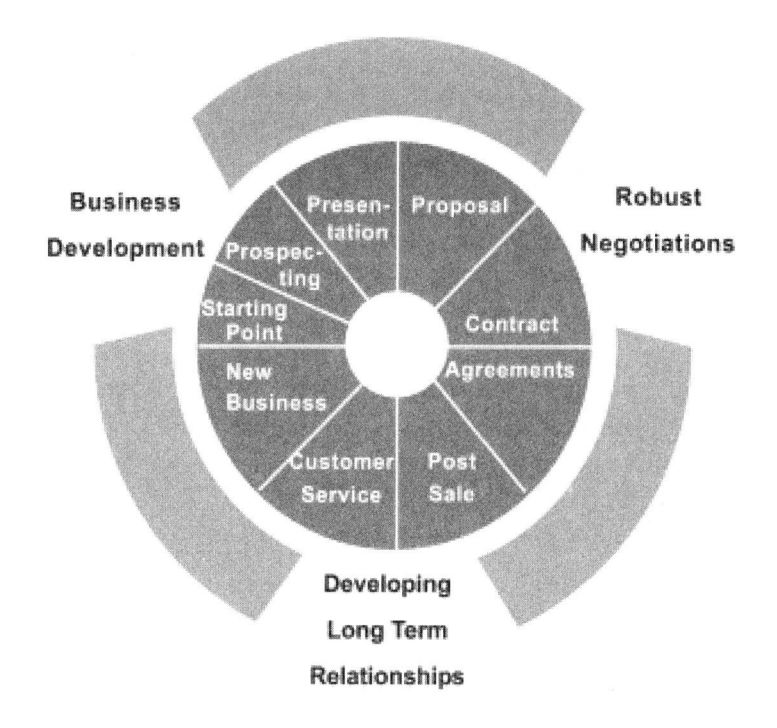

Diagram I.2 The Virtuous Circle and Synergy of Negotiation and the Multiple Phases of Business Development

I.3 Robust Negotiations

The concept of a robust negotiation is defined by the following characteristics:

- Clear vision of the parties,
- Clear objectives, all in the same direction,
- Cooperative work team,
- Maximum of three visits and closing.

On the contrary, the marathon negotiation is defined as the one whose characteristics are:

- Multiple visits to the client,
- Lack of objectives,
- Frustrating,
- Chaotic.

Think of a negotiation between a man and a woman. In this case, the negotiation might be a marathon for both parties, since what one likes, the other may dislike. What one sees in a certain form, the other sees differently, just as if we were negotiating with someone from a different culture or maybe even from a different planet (Gray, 1992). At times it seems as if we hold our conversations on different "wavelengths", for example, if we communicate that we "want it in red", they may tell us they "want it in green". It can become frustrating, especially if we are talking about the same thing in a different manner, and we do not understand one another.

How many times, as you try to explain something to your husband or wife, do they answer with different words, affirming what has been said? Nonetheless, it is perceived as a contradiction. This doesn't mean that if the counterpart is a man, a robust negotiation is guaranteed, and if it is a woman, it will be a marathon negotiation. There are men that produce marathon negotiations and women that guarantee a robust negotiation. We offer this example only to illustrate the concepts of robust and marathon negotiations. The extreme of these negotiations is when they become endless. On the other hand, there are projects that are of marathon nature and that require multiple robust negotiations with multiple agreements along the way.

It's important to have an established routine to review our everyday and strategic negotiations. Everyday negotiations, as the name suggests, are the ones we conduct with our families, coworkers and clients every single day, around the clock. Strategic negotiations are characterized by making a mark on the journey to success of the negotiator.

The balance of our negotiations consists in questioning ourselves on a daily basis about the negotiations we have in our briefcase: How many are robust? How many are the marathon kind? And, how many are endless? The ideal habit would be to put this reflection in practice once a day or at least once a week, and as a result, steer our efforts to the areas that need more support and stop investing resources in negotiations that are seen as long term ones or appear to be endless.

For a negotiation to become robust and efficient, we require having a global vision of the negotiation, understanding the client, his needs, the specific business opportunity, the decision makers, the process for decision making, the competition, the market, and a deep knowledge of our products and services. Moreover, we need to understand what follows in the relationship with the client after the sale is made. What is the payment process? How good is the client at paying? What is the culture of his business?, etc.

I.4 Long Term Client Relationships

Our concern in offering new terms such as: robust negotiations, marathon negotiations, as well as the interest of promoting cooperative negotiations (Nierenberg, 1995; Fisher, Ury and Patton, 1991), where both parties win, stems from the need to sustain long term client relationships. On the contrary, if in your negotiations you have no need to sustain a relationship with your client, the best strategy of negotiation is the competitive one.

Let's review the following example.

You are driving down a road and periodically see fruit stands selling oranges. There is not just one orange salesman, but one every 1500 feet. Every 1500 feet you find a salesman selling oranges. These salesmen are standing on the edge of the road waiting for clients to pull over and buy a bag of oranges. And let's say that, after you have driven several miles, you notice that the price for a bag of oranges ranges between $1 and $1.50 each. You decide to buy a bag of oranges and ask one of the sellers, "Excuse me, Sir. How much is a bag of oranges?" and he replies, "$1.50 a bag, and if you buy two, I can let you have them at $1 each." Now, since you consider that a fair price, you decide to purchase them, because in your experience, these cost between $1 and $1.50 each. You buy two bags of oranges at $1 each, and on your way home, a few miles further down the road you see that there are other salesmen, selling bags of oranges at 75¢ a bag. And you think, "What a fool! I didn't even try to lower the price of the salesman with the oranges, and he got away with it." While it is true that you may have felt intimidated with the power of legitimacy of a price tag (Cohen, 1982) or the price you had seen on the market, this probably prevented you from asking for a better price, because at the moment when you bought the bag, you had convinced yourself that the fair price was between $1 and $1.50 each. The point I want to make with this example, is that we are talking about a short-term negotiation, where the salesman with oranges is transparent to the client, which means that if you were to return to this salesman, you'd never find him. They all look alike and you probably don't even remember his name. In this type of negotiation, the competitive negotiation is completely justified.

When selling services to repetitive clients, where we want to build long-term relationships, we can't become like the orange salesman, or our clients won't see us again. We will become invisible, and they will never come back for another sale, since the importance of the product is way above that of the service, or the person.

In fact, another important factor in the purchase of the oranges is that the client purchased them. The salesman did not go out to sell them. This is in contrast to our current sales of products and services, where it is the goal to go out, sell and develop relationships with clients who will eventually provide repeat business.

> "The wind of adversity never blows over the kingdom of wisdom."
>
> Persian Proverb

Chapter II

Once I wanted to get a quote to send some material overseas. The country of destination didn't have an infrastructure for reliable shipping. By calling the country's embassy in the States, I received a service provider referral for Country Express. Country Express' general manager is Tom. Tom didn't ask us what our real need was. He assumed that we were just looking for a quote, and that was it. So he quoted $3.25 per kilogram of material and a 2 to 3-week delivery time for door-to-door shipping of goods. This price included customs and border crossing fees.

The dollar amount didn't tell me anything at that time, especially since I was not familiar with process of sending materials to that country. I had no baseline knowledge of what was a fair market value for this service. So I told Tom that I would think about it and get back to him shortly. I was really looking for the cheapest way to send the goods, and I didn't care much about the delivery time. Time wasn't an issue, but cost was. Tom didn't realize it, and didn't bother to ask me questions to find out my needs. He limited himself to providing just a standard service quote.

To make sure I was getting a good deal, I called an airline cargo company to get their quote. The airline price was $3.10 per kilogram for 2-day, door-to-door delivery. The same scope of work was included on this quote as was in Tom's estimate.

Since the embassy recommended Country Express, I called Tom back and mentioned that I had a quote of $3.10 per kilogram of material delivered by air in two days time. I requested an explanation of why his quote was $3.25 per kilogram for a service requiring up to 3 weeks. He offered to match the quote and send it by air as well. I told him that I didn't care about the delivery time, but I did care about getting the least expen-

33

sive alternative. He suggested sending it by sea, as originally quoted, and giving us a break at $1.38 per pound. This sounded like an excellent deal – a much lower figure. Now we were getting somewhere. Then I ran the conversion from pounds to kilograms and found the price discount was only $0.05 per kilogram.

At this moment, trust in the service provider was lost. He didn't build trust in the buying cycle, and, in fact, he was building distrust. First, he didn't bother to understand our need. Secondly, he quoted us a high bid which was lowered only when confronted with a reference value for the same service. Finally, he manipulated the negotiation with a change of variables by quoting price per pounds instead of per kilogram. At this point, I was willing to pay a higher price in order to deal with a service provider I could trust.

There are several dimensions in a negotiation. Initially, price was my primary variable of interest, but things changed during the process of negotiation.

A skillful negotiator will approach each deal knowing that price is not the only element under consideration.

The 6 P's of Robust Negotiation

"The future belongs to those who believe in the beauty of their dreams." - "Eleanor Roosevelt

This chapter contains the following topics:

II.1 The Dimensions of Negotiation

II.2 The 6 P's of Negotiation
  i **Person**
  ii **Product**
  iii **Problem**
  iv **Process**
  v **Power**
  vi **Prognosis**

II.1 The Dimensions of Negotiation

In real life, there are three or more dimensions that describe the behavior of things. The phenomenon of real life is modeled mathematically with more precision when several dimensions are used in the model. When negotiating, in similar fashion, if we negotiate in a single dimension (i.e. cost), we gain at the expense of other parameters. Before entering into a negotiation, we must be capable of visualizing the dimensions of the negotiation we are about to carry out, while also making a mental review as to what points are negotiable, and which are non-negotiable because they are giving without asking (see Diagram II.1). We also recommend making a list of priorities, followed by the fundamental question, "Are we are interested in a relationship with the other party, or solely interested in the matter at hand, both or neither?"

Non-negotiable

Negotiable
Area of Key Focus

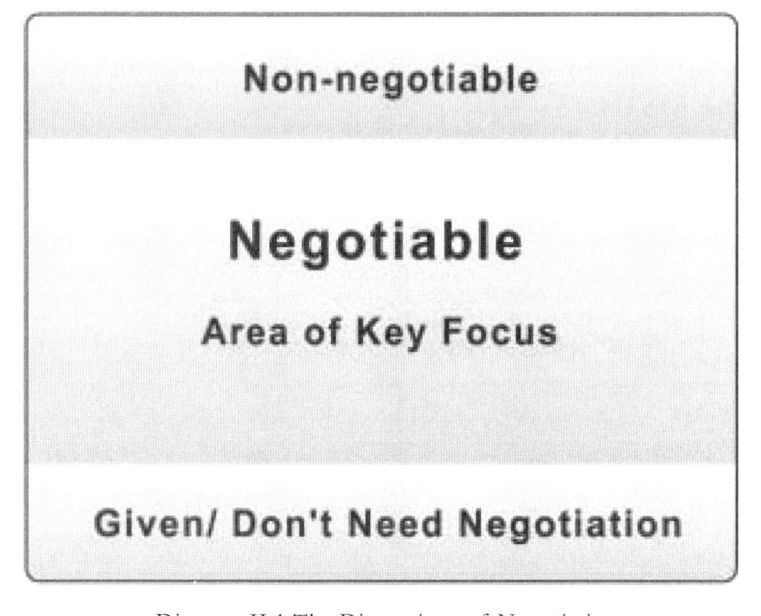

Given/ Don't Need Negotiation

Diagram II.1 The Dimensions of Negotiation

Once we have pointed out the priorities, what is and what isn't negotiable and determined if we are interested in a long term relationship with the client, we can start to design the fabric of our game board and commence analyzing what our best move will be.

In sports, one team losses and the other team wins. In Game Theory of Mathematics, we can select several moves in which both sides win. It is not only what you are negotiating but how you are negotiating that is important.

This is only half of the story. For the other half, we must do our homework with our counterpart, understanding where he's coming from, what his aspirations are and what he expects from us.

With this, we can proceed to design our general strategy of negotiation and project, and if it will be a competitive or co-operative negotiation. An alternative is to transfer the move to the counterpart avoiding the negotiation altogether (see Diagram II.2).

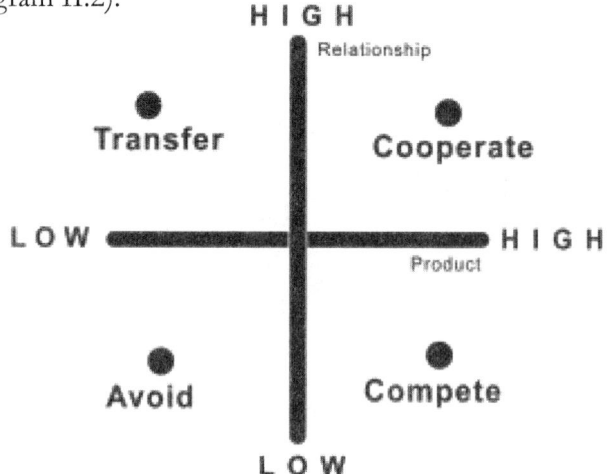

```
              HIGH
           Relationship
     ●                    ●
  Transfer            Cooperate

LOW ━━━━━━━━━┼━━━━━━━━━ HIGH
                Product

     ●                    ●
   Avoid              Compete

              LOW
```

Diagram II.2 Negotiation Strategies according to the Importance of the Relationship with the Person and the Importance of the Product by Savage, Blair and Sorenson, 1989

II.2 The 6 P's of Negotiation

Let's go into the details by breaking down the negotiation into the 6 P's, so both parties can win. The 6 P's are: **Person, Process, Product, Problem, Power** and **Prognosis**.

If we analyze the 6 P's of negotiation, we can have a better understanding of which phase is a "bottleneck" or what we have yet to learn in our process. For example, perhaps the "bottleneck" is not understanding the reasoning or the business model of a foreign culture. If we analyze that within the framework of the 6 P's, it will help us to quickly determine where the problem or the opportunity lies.

The **Person** (with his cultural differences, egos, attitudes, interests and behaviors) is an important part of the game of negotiation — this plus our understanding of the aspirations and psychology the counterpart is using.

Both the **Process** and its parts invite us to reflect: What sequence do we use to start the **Process** of negotiation? What is the frame of reference and action to be used?

Many times the **Problem** is solved by changing its frame of reference.

The **Product** and its benefits tied into the needs of the client are essential parts of the negotiation. Even more important is the detailed knowledge of the characteristics of the **Product**. If we are not dealing with the negotiation of a **Product**, such as in a conflict or a dispute, then the **Problem** applies. That is to say, the **Problem** that we are about to face or solve is in itself, the subject of the negotiation.

Power and its sources are important parts of the art of negotiation. There are sources that generate **Power** such as information, time, precedent, knowledge, a good relationship with the other party (Cohen, 1982; Stark, 1995; Karras, 1992), etc. We show the 6 P's of negotiation in Diagram II.3.

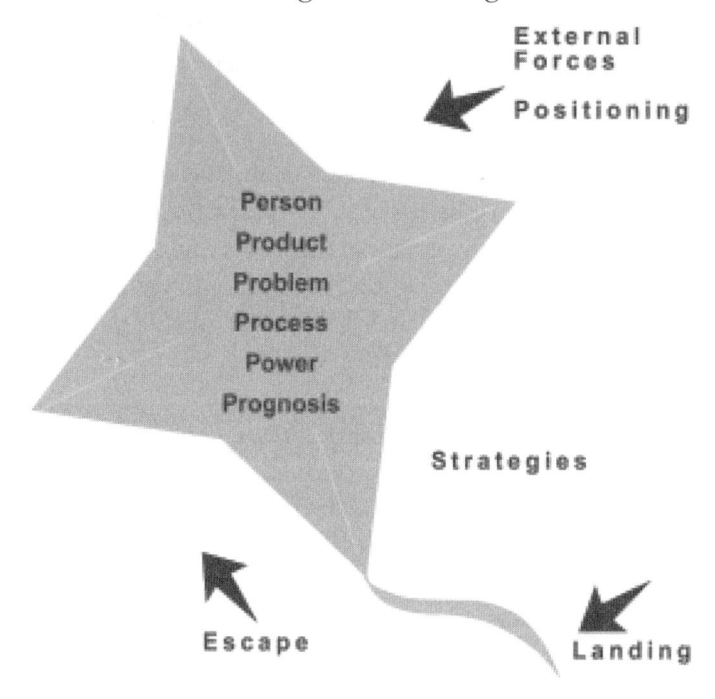

External Forces
Positioning
Person
Product
Problem
Process
Power
Prognosis
Strategies
Escape
Landing

Diagram II.3 The 6 P's of Negotiation according to CHAMOUN

Now let's see what both players have to do to win at the game of negotiation.

On some occasions we lose because we play with the wrong people or do not understand the needs of the players on the other team. Despite our knowledge of the game, we lose, because we are playing the wrong game.

The game of negotiation is complex and differs from football because there are several ways both teams can win.

Using this analogy, let's walk through the process.

Sometimes we pick the right game (the strategies), play with the right people (good chemistry, a compatible business model, spirit of cooperation of the parties), but we don't use the right ball and our shoes are uncomfortable, so we lose the game (**The context**).

To ensure our victory, it is not only necessary to play with the right people (**Person**), pick the right game (**Process**) and the right playing field (**Product**). It is also important to consider if our prognosis is a current one that includes the external forces of the market.

There are other factors that, according to their scale, may lead to the success or total loss of the game. These include, but are not limited to: 1) the imbalance of power and 2) the external forces (Market) previously described.

For example, let's suppose that we are in the right game, with the right players, except that the players of one of the teams have extreme superior power over the other. This perception of power might loom so large in the minds of the opposing team that even if they are better players, they will be intimidated and lose. It might happen that an external force intervenes, such as a change in the climate, that affects the performance of one team and not the other. As a result, one of them will suffer total failure. In this same scenario, there might be external market forces present in the game of negotiation and, no matter how robust or efficient the negotiation conducted by the parties has been, it will freeze the result just the same.

Let's say we have closed the **Deal** with a client in two visits. We have come to an agreement, understanding in detail his needs, covering all those points in the proposal and have efficiently closed the deal. Excellent! As defined in the book *Business Development*, we have achieved a robust negotiation. If suddenly the deal falls through due to "external forces", we would define this as a "frozen robust negotiation."

In the case of the sale of consulting services, while consulting firm "Y" was trying to close a deal with client "X", "X" did not count on enough staff to allow "Y" to offer the consulting at that specific time. Let's suppose they were short on staff due to a market situation that made it difficult to hire personnel at the company. The robust negotiation would continue to be frozen until the personnel had been hired. In this case, we failed with the last P, since we did not make a correct **Prognosis** according to the client's capabilities.

Remember that in the game of negotiation there are 6 important points to consider.

First, the **Person** (the players), their needs, culture, aspirations, expectations, education, socioeconomic level, etc.

Second, the **Process** (the game). How are we going to play? In what sequence? Who are we passing the ball to? What strategy will we follow? What strategy will the other team follow? What are their classic moves? Which plays are atypical? (Breslin and Rubin, 1999; Nierenberg, 1995; Pruitt, 1991; Raiffa, 2000; Walton, 1965; Watkins, 2002; Young, 1994; Zartman, 1991)

Third, the **Product** (what is being negotiated, the subject). Commonly this is the main focus of the negotiating parties. "Product" could be the scope of work being negotiated.

Fourth, the **Power**, the perception one team has of the other (strengths and weaknesses). It must be considered that there are several sources of power: information, time, precedent (Cohen, 1982; Stark, 1995; Karras, 1992), etc.

The fifth P, **Problem** applies when we are negotiating conflicts or disputes (Fisher, 1989, 1996; HBR, 2000; Pruitt, 1986; Stone, Patton and Heen, 2000; Susskind and Field, 1996; Ury, 1991, 2000).

In addition to the first 5 P's of negotiation, **Person**, **Product**, **Problem**, **Process** and **Power**, there are external forces that might have an unavoidable effect on the other and must be considered in the sixth P, **Prognosis**: Capitalizing on adequate and current information, we will ensure the success of the negotiation.

We will proceed to describe these in more detail.

II.2.i Person

Keep in mind that behind every institution, firm, corporation or family business there are persons who have their own interests in the negotiation underway. We will represent these persons with the first P of negotiation. In the book **Business Development,** we define the CHAMOUN Models of Types of Salesmen©2003, which we present here in Diagrams II.4 and II.5. This model helps us evaluate ourselves as salespersons before different types of clients and also to evaluate our purchasers. The idea is to understand the characteristics of the salesman or purchaser in regard to the client/vendor relationship and have an objective view of the Person we are negotiating with.

Ask yourself: "How many people are behind a decision? Who influences them? What moves each one?" A client, while making a certain purchase, may have a personal interest that influences his decision taking, whether 1) he might get promoted, 2) he likes the product, 3) he trusts the product or service, 4) it awakens memories or arouses feelings of nostalgia, belonging, etc. When a client makes a purchasing decision, he must often sell it to his "internal clients" (his employees, etc.) and convince them of the reason supporting the purchase of a service or product.

It has been proven that a great number of people make a purchasing decision based on previous experiences, trust and emotions, among other things. It's important to fully understand "what" motivates each person involved in the purchasing process. We must ask the client, "What is your need? What do you like about your current suppliers? What is the profile of your ideal service provider?" We must start by creating a good relationship and investing resources in that business relationship long before we talk about our products and services.

A high percentage of frustrated negotiations have had to do with the persons we are negotiating with. Maybe they "don't like us," or no chemistry exists, or we haven't found the right approach, or we simply don't understand them. Above all, in the cultural environment we live in, there are people who prefer to incur a loss, so long as someone else doesn't win.

How often do we find ourselves in the need to negotiate with someone difficult? What do we do if the person in charge of the most important negotiation of the year is arrogant, rude, egocentric and bad mannered? What do the experts recommend if the client offends us, attacks us or yells at us?

It's a difficult question, and it's more difficult still to control our own impulses and reactions. Nonetheless, the answer is a simple one. We must surprise our clients, contrary to our inclination to counterattack, and maintain self control

As explained by Dr. William Ury (Harvard professor and author of "The Third Party", "Getting Past No", co-author of best seller "Getting to Yes". See references.), we must first control our own internal reactions of anger, jealousy and envy.

Then, we must understand why our client is reacting in such an aggressive way. What is the problem? What is the interest behind the position? We must learn to separate the person from the problem (Fisher, Ury and Patton, 1991), to be gentle with the person and tough on the problem.

Often the difficulty in separating the person from the problem comes from a cultural effect. In Latin and Oriental cultures it is very difficult to separate the person from the problem. It is less difficult to do so in the Anglo Saxon culture, especially with males. Maybe these differences are due to the educational, social, legal and economic systems that a person is exposed to since childhood. Whatever the cause may be, we must learn the best from other cultures and apply that, as in the case of not taking work issues personally. For example, if someone at the office mentions that your work is poorly done, you will surely take it personally. Let's learn to accept things objectively. On the other hand, if you have a problem with the person who is negotiating, first solve the personal problem, and then follow up with the matter of negotiation. Let some time go by so the other person "cools off" his feelings of anger, and then he can reenter the negotiation with a clear mind.

Going back to the aggressive client, we recommend you focus on thinking of something else when the client is offending you. Let your imagination fly, forget the problem, concentrate on the person, and try to understand why he is behaving this way. Take your time in asking, "Why are you angry? I really want to understand the reason" Give the client the opportunity to vent. Don't try to fix the issue at that moment, since you don't have an objective mind in either party. Devote your time to trying to understand the problem in depth. It's important that you give yourself time to think of plausible solutions (logical and possible).

The following day, after the client has "said his piece", offer alternatives that satisfy the needs of the client. The moral of the story is that we must first think about the counterpart, then about the counterpart and finally, about the counterpart, finding out what he needs and then offering a solution in which both parts win (see "The Art of Negotiation" by Dr. Gerard I. Nierenberg).

Another factor that may affect the result of the negotiation between the parties is the psychological anchor — the manipulation by way of lies or dishonesty on behalf of one of the parties. Making a high priced first offer, in the case of a salesman or one too low, in the case of the buyer, affects the range of discounts of both parties. The psychological anchor in the minds of the persons negotiating may be affected by that first offer. For example, if someone is selling a product and the buyer asks what discount he can get. If the salesman says 20%, he may lose the power of negotiation. If, to the contrary, the salesman asks the buyer what discount he is used to receiving and the buyer says a 10% discount, the salesman has obtained a 10% leverage factor in his favor over the previous case, without providing information on his range of discounts from the start.

By this I don't mean to say that it's detrimental to be the first one to make an offer. Someone has to break the ice, but if you open the negotiation, be prepared before making an offer. The conclusion of this story is that the Person with whom we are negotiating plays an important role and is considered here as the first P of negotiation.

II.2.ii Product

It's frequently observed that salesmen of products and services commit the same mistakes by letting themselves be led

- Service
- Strategy
- Methodology

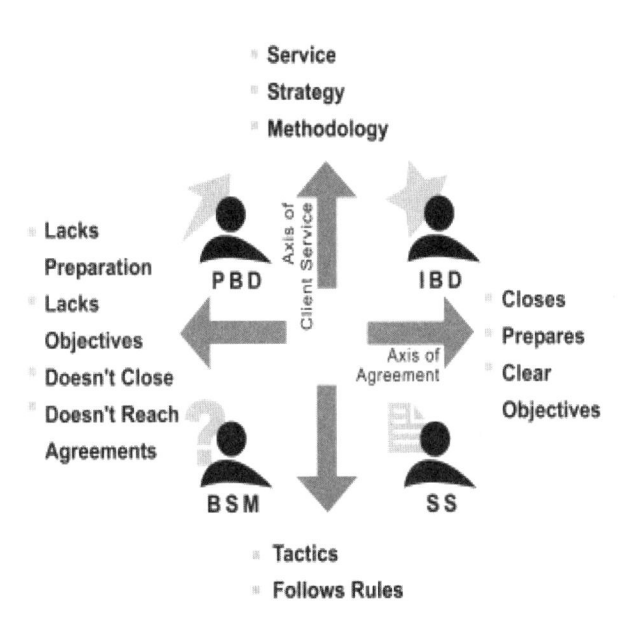

- Lacks Preparation
- Lacks Objectives
- Doesn't Close
- Doesn't Reach Agreements

PBD   IBD

Axis of Client Service

Axis of Agreement

- Closes
- Prepares
- Clear Objectives

BSM   SS

- Tactics
- Follows Rules

Diagram II.4 The Person and the 4 Types of CHAMOUN Salesmen

PBD	Potential Business Developer
IBD	Ideal Business Developer
SS	Simple Salesman
BSM	Blank Slate Mind

Types of CHAMOUN Salesmen

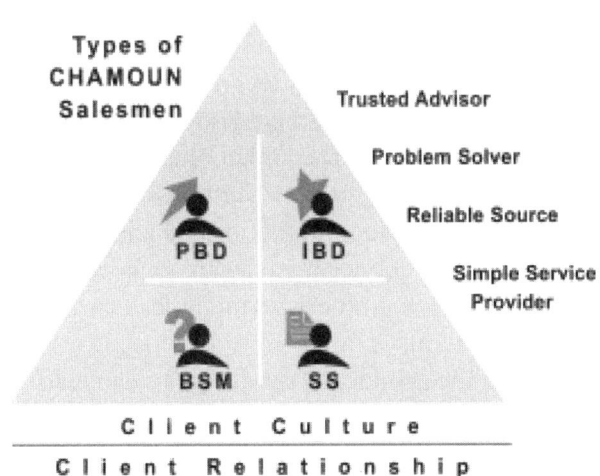

- Trusted Advisor
- Problem Solver
- Reliable Source
- Simple Service Provider

PBD   IBD
BSM   SS

Client Culture
Client Relationship

Diagram II.5 Relationship by Type of CHAMOUN Salesman with the Client/Vendor Relationship

47

by the "benefits of the product or service" they sell. The typical salesman receives training on the characteristics and technical details of the product and service to be sold. The sales manager may declare more than once that his product sells itself and that it's a question of hiring star salesmen and only training them on the "benefits of the product or service". Though it's true that to sell something, it is essential to have an in depth knowledge of that which is being sold.

Experience has proven that we must also train sales people in the skills and knowledge of sales and negotiations.

Let's not assume that only the knowledge of the "benefits of the product or service" are of high importance. It is just as important to find out what it is that makes the client "tick" in regard to the benefits of the products or services.

To master a product or service, we recommend you:

- Learn about it fully, including its limitations,
- Convert the limitations of the product or service into strengths,
- Avoid offering excess information that will show the limitations of the product or service,
- Be honest with the client and show him, at a convenient time, the limitations of the product or service that might cause him problems in the future,
- Do not mention limitations if the limitation of the product or service is irrelevant or doesn't affect the client -(Doing otherwise might lead to a bad perception),
- Keep the product or service up to date with the needs of the market,
- Have knowledge of substitute products or services that are a direct or indirect competition,
- Know of complimentary products or services.

A product has a "useful life". A service as well as a product may be reengineered to continue in the market and expand its product cycle. Ask yourself, how are your products or services positioned? What negotiation strategies must you use? Who is your competition? How is your competition performing? Where do you see your products or services in a few years? Analyze your product and service well, and we'll have another guaranteed P (Product) in the negotiation. In summary, consider the following for the product and service:

- Knowledge of what is being sold or bought,
- Characteristics vs. benefits,
- Analysis of the priorities,
- A deep understanding of the client's needs.

II.2.iii Problem

The negotiation of problems differs from that of products. In the first case, there are feelings between the parties that do not necessarily exist in the negotiation of products. What is most recommendable for this type of negotiation is to obtain the assistance of a third party. This third party may serve the function of an arbitrator, facilitator or impartial mediator. The objective of these negotiations is very different from the negotiation of products and services. The objective of the parties might be to: 1) avoid jail, 2) avoid lawsuits, 3) avoid union strikes, 4) pay increases, etc.

This type of negotiation involves the theory of decision taking within different scenarios and is merely a process for the resolution of problems among the parties.

Ideally, all the efforts of negotiation should focus on the why of the problem and in evaluating the different alternatives to the non-agreement between the parties. (BATNA, Dr. Roger Fisher and Dr. William Ury, "Getting to Yes", see reference.)

This way we can plan the negotiation better. Let's suppose that a person is suing a corporation. The alternatives for the person, if there is no agreement with the corporation, may be: 1) that the person pays his attorney's fees, 2) that the company pay the minimum damages to the person. The alternatives for the corporation, if there is no agreement with the person, may be: 1) bad publicity, 2) temporary closing of the offices, etc. In this example, the "BATNAs" (Best Alternative to the Negotiated Agreement, Fisher and Ury), are such that the one with the most to lose is the corporation, since if it does not reach an agreement with the person, it risks the temporary closing of the corporation. Here the company should determine how much this closing could cost and the probability of it happening. Then perhaps, if what the employee is asking is below the cost of the alternative to the non-agreement, there is a space for negotiation. If we know our alternatives and the other parties', we can determine the range of discount between the parties and plan an effective negotiation that way.

Typically, these negotiations deal with several issues and are conducted with several parties. Price might be the least important point, and what we have to focus on is the impact that every alternative might have on the parties involved. For this reason, we should carry out an analysis of the impact of each alternative and select the best one for the parties.

Another example of a problem negotiation is the renegotiation of a contract with clients who are upset after having purchased a service or product. To avoid this situation, we recommend you describe the scope of each project in detail, clearly saying in the contract between the parties what it includes and what is not included. This is similar to when you go to a sales seminar, and the advertising mentioned it included a coffee break. It would be best to explain that the coffee break does not include sandwiches and cookies, and only includes coffee and the break (recess). If you don't mention what is not included, the expectations of our client would turn to disappointment.

Let's try to avoid the renegotiation of contracts and misunderstandings with the client, by educating him and "walking the talk".

	Problems	Products
Objective	Avoid Arguments	Improve Position on Price
Alternative to Agreement	Jail, Court	Find Another Supplier
Process	Mediation	Negotiation
Typical Parts of the Process	Referee, Judge, Filing Parties	Buyer and Vendor

Chart 2.1 Some Examples of Differences between Problem and Product Negotiations

II.2.iv Process

"Negotiation is a collection of causes and conditions that repeatedly coincide to transform the initial interest into the final terms, with the objective of improving the parties' positions in time, cost and scope." - Dr. Habib Chamoun-Nicolás.

We often think that negotiations among the parties should be quick and efficient. If we understand the needs of the persons, the products and problems, we will find that they move slowly and take longer than we expected.

Like a good cake that takes a while to bake, so does a good negotiation. Time requirements depend on the process and the parties involved, who, in the end, are the ones who make things happen or not. In the case of multiple suppliers who manufacture a product where each vendor adds value in the supply chain, a vendor who becomes a bottleneck will delay the process and, as a result, the negotiation.

Another factor in the process is the flow of information between the negotiating parties. There are bureaucratic and corporate organizations that, as a policy, demand certain procedures for the flow of information, which is a limitation in the negotiation process. For example, if we are negotiating with a company that requires certain paperwork before having a conversation about negotiation, let's send the information ahead of us! Let's research what documentation we need before we begin. Prepare all the copies and forms, and we will gain time in the process. Let's learn to manage the process and not the persons!

Research the steps that are included in the client's corporate process. That way you can be sure to prepare the information in a timely manner and in the form that your internal or external client is used to handling.

For example, if you are applying for a type of permit and are unfamiliar with the process, (the correct information flow and the rules), you will become easily frustrated.

Otherwise if you are familiar with the process, you can visualize several options before the other party and speed up the closing.

How often are we unable to obtain what we want because we are unfamiliar with the process, as is the case of a bid negotiation with certain game rules? If you have ever participated in the preparation of a proposal for services, you will have noticed that many times it is not the price, nor the quality, nor the payment or technical terms that disqualify us. What disqualifies us are the little details in the rules of the game, such as: 1) not having gone to a visit at the work site, or perhaps 2) not having delivered the proposal on time because the flight was late.

The process of negotiation helps establish the rules of the game and moreover, helps us visualize the different game moves we have as options. Understanding from the start that there is a negotiation process is a big advantage. Afterwards we ask ourselves, "Who are the parties in the process, and what strategies should we follow? In what sequence? How does an action with one of the parties in the negotiation affect others in the process? What is our best move within this context?" The parts of the process are everything that surrounds the negotiation, from the number of participants, the number of issues to negotiate, the layers of the negotiation (what is negotiable and what is not) to the context in which the negotiation will be carried out, and others.

We divide the negotiation process into four phases: Pre-Negotiation, Rough Negotiation, Fine Negotiation and Post-Negotiation.

Pre-Negotiation

The main basis of this phase is to start to understand what the real interest behind the position of each of the parties is. For this purpose, we recommend you question the parties creatively until you find the real interest.

This phase primarily involves listening. Both parties have to be researched in depth. Questions are made without commitments. Both parties explore and brainstorm. What would happen if…? What would be the points to surrender? Criticism of ideas is not recommended at this phase to avoid stopping the flow of ideas. In other words, this phase is a simulation of the negotiation, of inventing options and expanding the possibilities of reaching an agreement.

We recommend:

- Actively promote brainstorming,
- Interview the parties that will form the negotiation team,
- Get to know the parties who will intervene ahead of time.

Rough Negotiation

It's typical that in this phase, the majority of successful negotiators will concede on most of the points that are unimportant as an initial strategy and in the next phase concede practically nothing at all. This is not a general rule, because there are those that choose to use the opposite strategy, conceding on very few points in the beginning and changing this position in the end.

We recommend:

- Understanding the position of the other party,
- Continuing to ask questions to uncover the interest,
- Giving options while asking,
- Having the creativity to invent options,
- Comparing against the standards of the industry in question,
- Understanding the human factor,
- Having alternatives (Plan B, in case Plan A fails),
- Identifying the client's important points,
- Proactively listening,
- Leaving the most difficult points for the negotiation.

Fine Negotiation

This is the phase of the little details that make the negotiation happen or not. The efficiency of the negotiation is going to depend on this stage.
We recommend:

- Reviewing who the attorneys are for both sides,
- Negotiating the most difficult points,
- Not pressuring yourself,
- Reaching a preliminary agreement.

Post-Negotiation

This phase is the one that deals with the paperwork, the first stone and formalization.

We recommend:

- Wrapping things up adequately - (Everyone wants to get in on the start, yet they forget about the filing),
- Finalizing the last details,
- Maintaining a file on the lessons learned for future negotiations,
- Conducting interviews with the client in order to determine what areas can be improved and what errors were made during the negotiation process.

II.2.v Power

There are many sources of power in the literature of negotiation(Cohen, 1982; Stark, 1995; Karras, 1992): the power of legitimacy, and the price tags, among others. The fact that some products have a price tag gives them power. Some people think twice before negotiating and asking for a discount and consequently, lose power by being unable to sell at a higher price than the price tag. This is one of the reasons why, especially in the service industry, we recommend not putting a price tag on your services, since the prepared client will surely ask for a discount on the established price and it's very difficult to negotiate a price to a higher level. This means that, if you sell something at $10 and offer a 10% discount and they buy your product at $9, the next time it will be harder to sell it to the client at $12. There are several reasons why. One is that the client expects a price below $9 the next time he buys it, and other one is that you started at $10. Selling at $12 is possible, but difficult. In this case, you must remind the client that the 10% discount was only on the first purchase, so as not to establish a precedent; hence we can use this as another source of power. When we sell something well, we have to establish a precedent, so that in the future we have "high", "fair" values as a reference and not the average values of the market.

Experience is another source of power. An experienced negotiator may intimidate the counterpart just because he stands to win. Another maneuver of power may be sending a client to the competition so he can make comparisons and be 100% convinced. This strategy only works so long as we have an added value and believe that the client himself will return after having proof of it.

In essence, everything that gives him confidence or that justifies the purchase to the client is a source of power. If the way we dress, act, speak, present, propose and deliver our products is consistent with the client's perception of us, we will generate power of negotiation.

In other words, the coherence and consistency of the words and actions of the negotiator with the client are the foundation on which the relationship of trust with our clients is built. A distrustful client is the best friend of our competitors. This is why it is important to analyze the power of negotiation by understanding how the other party perceives us. What are our strengths and weaknesses from the client's point of view? Ask your client, once you have developed a business relationship: How do you see us? What would you like us to change? What do we do right that you'd like to see us do again for you? What are the characteristics of your ideal vendor? We have to be realistic, too. We can't give the client everything he wants, or he'll lead us to the poor house.

Other sources of power mentioned in the literature (see references: "You Can Negotiate Anything" by Herb Cohen) are:

- Information,
- Perception,
- Time,
- Imbalance of Power (Extremes).

II.2.vi Prognosis

This P implies risk. Know that there is always the possibility, albeit a small one, of not reaching an agreement with the other party. Try to understand how to minimize that risk whenever possible.

There will always be "hidden" reasons why the client won't carry out the purchase with us. Sometimes they are quite obvious, as in the cases of price competition, quality, delivery time or technical questions. Not having made a good prognosis of our closing might have been a result of not knowing the "hidden truth" of the reason or motive of the purchase. Perhaps the "hidden truth" is that the client doesn't trust our services, or he feels an obligation to another service provider, or his "gut feeling" told him he shouldn't buy from us, or maybe there are multiple reasons.

The intention of the prognosis is that we become aware that it is not enough to know the other P's of negotiation. There is always a risk beyond our control, and that may have a lot to do with the external forces of the market.

The lesson learned is that we must understand our clients' market to see where it is going and ask ourselves, "How do we help them get to where they are going with our products and services?" I assure you that if you are able to give your clients the answer to this question, they will become strategic accounts. After seeing examples of the 6 P's of negotiation, we can appreciate that they can be useful tools for putting things in context and being able to project what we can do with each one and thus, find a solution that is convenient for all parties.

The 6 P's of negotiation are the motor behind **Deal**.

Steps to Follow to Determine the Strategy of Negotiation

After evaluating the **Person**, the **Problem** or **Product**, the **Process**, the **Power** of the parties, and the environment, we can make the **Prognosis** and dictate what strategy we should follow, as seen previously in Diagram II.2 and here in Diagram II.6 (Savage, Blair and Sorensen, 1989).

The strategy of negotiation will depend on the importance of the client/vendor relationship and the importance of the subject of the negotiation (see Diagram II.2).

The veracity of the strategy of negotiation will depend on the validity of the previous analysis based on the six P's of negotiation and on the good preparation of the parties.

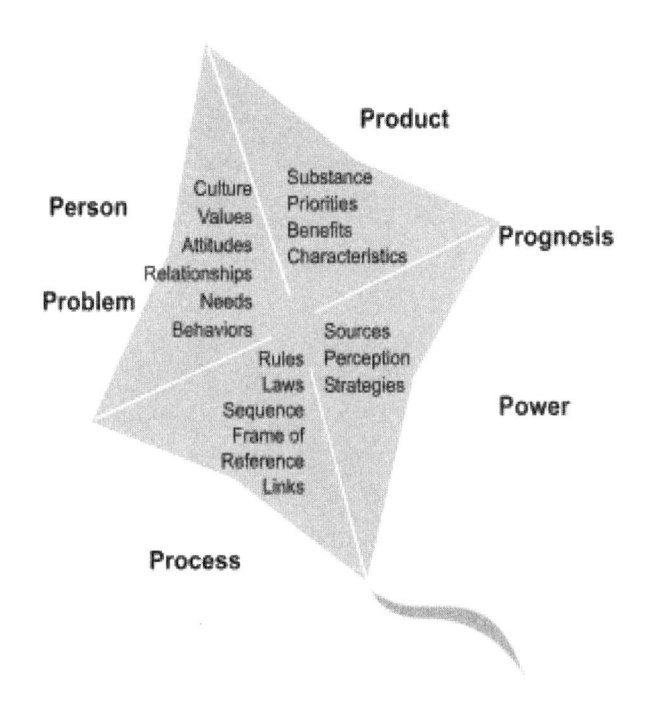

Diagram II.6 Summary of the 6 P's of Negotiation (Savage, Blair and Sorensen, 1989).

"True wisdom is not the deep knowledge of remote, unused, obscure and subtle things, but rather that of everyday things that lie before our very eyes." -Milton

Chapter III

One beautiful sunny day I was driving my car past a country club golf course on a busy street in Mexico. All of the sudden, I had to stop at a red light, and a car hit me from behind. We both pulled over to assess the damage. The driver that hit my car was a medical doctor named Jose. Jose, assumed all responsibility, and we called the insurance companies to do their due diligence and pay the damages.

In Mexico, car insurance agents must file an on-the-scene report for auto claims. While waiting for the car insurance agents, Jose and I were developing rapport. He asked me what I did for a living. After I mentioned to him that I conducted business development and negotiation workshops, he replied, "How interesting. I am a medical doctor, and I am in the process of starting a new business. I need to develop my negotiation skills. As you know, medical doctors usually don't negotiate with patients." To that I added, "You don't. Your assistant does." He responded, "Could you help me?" I replied, "Definitely. As a matter of fact, I have an open enrollment negotiation workshop next month. If you register today, I will personally make a case study of your business opportunity." I added, "Now this incident is going to be less expensive. In fact, I have some information in my trunk. Let me get it for you." Before the insurance agent arrived to the accident scene, Jose had registered for the workshop. He had also initiated a successful business startup.

You never know when you are going to run into a business opportunity. Daily situations present opportunities. The ability to clearly see them and perform a robust negotiation is something we can learn. Be prepared to negotiate everywhere, and your power of negotiation will increase in any situation.

The Culture and 6 P's of Robust Negotiation

"Be awfully nice to them going up, because you're gonna meet them all coming down. " - Jimmy Durante

This chapter contains the following topics:

III.1 Culture and International Negotiation

III.2 The Culture and 6 P's

III.3 Global Vision of Negotiation

III.4 The Great Differences between Cultures as the Driving event of Negotiation. Without Differences, There is No Need to Negotiate

III.1 Culture and International Negotiation

Culture and Negotiation

Negotiation is an industry that is growing around the world, and not just because of conflicts between people of regions and countries. It is growing because of the possibility of collaboration and cooperation between parties from different latitudes. We negotiate because of the differences that exist in the way we think, feel and act. If those differences are unknown or are not analyzed and understood, it will be difficult to work, do business or even live in a country with people who think, feel and act differently from us.

We study the "culture" as an independent factor in the process of international negotiations. To be able to understand cultural differences, we must ask ourselves three questions:

- What is culture?
- What does culture affect more: the process of negotiation or the results?
- Why does culture affect the strategy of negotiation?

What is culture?

"Culture is a set of values, beliefs, norms, representations of reality or values shared by a group or society." We can say that it is a phenomenon that represents a group or area. Culture is a window that allows us to see and understand ways of communication and decision taking, to view values and beliefs, to analyze relationships with the government and institutions and to understand the history of societies.

There are no good, bad, inferior, or superior cultures. This is the real starting point for any analysis of negotiations among different cultures. Each culture is different in the way it views and perceives the world, its values and beliefs.

What does culture affect more: the process of negotiation or the results?

During negotiation, cultural differences affect the strategies to be used. Cultural differences can affect how difficult negotiations are or how long they take, but the result should not be affected.

Why does culture affect the strategy of negotiation?

One of the principal strategies of negotiation is that we should always seek to keep communication open and accompany it with respect and trust. When we study and analyze the culture, we seek to understand the components and norms that will make the interaction between persons easier. We analyze the norms, customs, behaviors, beliefs and religion, so we can sustain better communications. Culture envelops norms that facilitate social interaction, which directly affects the strategy of negotiation.

The Process of Negotiation between Different Cultures

The greatest challenge in international negotiations is the effective adaptation to the different cultures. This adaptation means continuing to move forward on unexpected roads and requires the comprehension of diverse cultures, perceptions, stereotypes and values.

Day to day, we can observe that a great number of negotiations fail because the parties ignore or underestimate their cultural differences.

Over the last few years, many studies have been conducted on culture and its dimensions and attitudes. Nonetheless, we should remember that generalizing and creating stereotypes is dangerous. There are always different individuals and subcultures that exist within the same country or even the same region.

One of the best studies on culture and its dimensions is the one conducted by the Dutchman Geert Hofstede in 1980 and updated in 1991. He defined four subdivisions to culture that help us explain and understand why and how people from different cultures act in the way they do.

Dimension 1: Distance from Power or Hierarchy

Cultures with a lot of distance from power accept the differences in power and status as being natural. The level of delegation or distribution of power/authority is low, and they tend to remove themselves or differentiate themselves as much as possible from those individuals that do not possess it. The leader/boss tends to have a paternal and authoritarian style. The elder superiors are generally more respected than the younger ones.

Cultures whose distance from power is small perceive the differences in power and status as unjust and artificial. Those who have power and authority tend to play it down, minimizing the differences between them and their subordinates. Power is distributed, and the degree of delegation is high. The style of direction tends to be participative and less authoritarian. Younger leaders are more admired than the elders.

Dimension 2: Individualism in the Face of Collectivism

In very individualistic cultures the smallest unit of survival is the individual. The needs of the individual take priority over those of the group. Independence and self confidence are valued and encouraged, and personal liberty and privacy are essentially desired and cannot be surrendered. Straightforwardness and direct style are rewarded. Saying what you mean is a sign of honesty. The issue to be dealt with prevails over the personal relationship.

In highly collectivist cultures the smallest unit of survival is the family (nuclear and extended: grandparents, siblings, aunts and uncles, cousins, nieces and nephews, etc.). The individual identity is, in great measure, derived from belonging to a group (family, clan, work team, etc) and from the role or part one plays. Group survival and success guarantee individual well being in such a way that by considering the needs and feelings of others the individual is protecting himself. Harmony and interdependence among the members of the group are valued and encouraged. You have to be careful with what you say and how you say it. Direct confrontations must be avoided. The personal relationship supersedes the issue to be dealt with.

Dimension 3: Masculinity Faced with Femininity

Masculinity refers to societies in which the social roles of both sexes are clearly differentiated. **In a strong masculine culture**, individuals feel motivated by material and professional achievements. Being successful means progressing and obtaining more responsibilities and profits. The possibility of obtaining success supersedes stability/ job and emotional security. If faced with the choice between work, relationships, or even family, the choice is work. The reason for living is work. Conflicts and disagreements are solved by confrontation and discussion. The typical masculine directive comes across as self-affirmation, aggressive, and active, with independent decision-making It is based more on information than on the opinions of the group.

Femininity refers to societies where the roles of both sexes shield each other. Both men and women must concern themselves with the quality of life and feelings. **In strong feminine cultures**, individuals feel motivated by a better quality of life in every aspect. More power and responsibility are not considered attractive per se. Success means being admired or loved in your surroundings. You work to live. Conflicts and disagreements are solved through compromise, consensus and negotiation. The typical feminine directive is more subtle, acts more by intuition than by information and entails more dialogue.

Dimension 4: Avoidance of Uncertainty

Avoidance of uncertainty reflects the level of anxiety present in a culture. **Cultures with a strong avoidance to uncertainty** tend to create a strategy that somehow allows them to reduce the uncertainty of the unknown. Issues such as job stability or financial security are a motive for anxiety. Assuming risks and fear of failure/ridicule are avoided as much as possible. Change is, by definition, threatening. What's different is dangerous, and what's new is not necessarily good or attractive. Traditions are respected and considered an effective guide for present and future action. There is a tendency towards bureaucracy and to increase and place a high value on control systems (accounting, etc.). Directors tend to be specialists rather than generalists and concern themselves with the details of their work. There is little delegation and scarce work mobility. Dissenters are seen as a threat.

In cultures with a weak avoidance of uncertainty individuals are not afraid to assume the risk of failure/ridicule. Experimentation is valued and rewarded. Change is stimulating and positive. What's different is attractive, and what's new is often considered better than what's old. Tradition is not appreciated per se, except where it is practical. Norms are scarce and are only established in case of absolute necessity. The directors tend to be generalists and occupy themselves more with strategic questions, leaving the details to others. There is a high level of delegation and job mobility. Dissent is accepted with a certain ease.

After reading the four dimensions of Hofstede, we see that it is expected that negotiation be affected by culture, and thus, it is very important to have a full understanding of its characteristics. There are other elements to consider such as the status of the persons, their social position, achievements, popularity, age, etc.

All the concepts we've been developing in this chapter are important in achieving a robust negotiation. Keep in mind that knowing about cultural differences does not mean we will try to imitate them or act on them. The knowledge of a national culture tells us a lot about the person, but an individual may represent a number of cultures, all of which can affect the way we negotiate.

Remember these key points when negotiating between different cultures. In order to achieve your objectives, you must understand that there are differences affecting the process and strategies of negotiation. Always respect and support the communication process.

III.2 Culture and the 6 P's

Culture has an effect that changes the form of the 6 P's of Negotiation (See Diagram III.1)

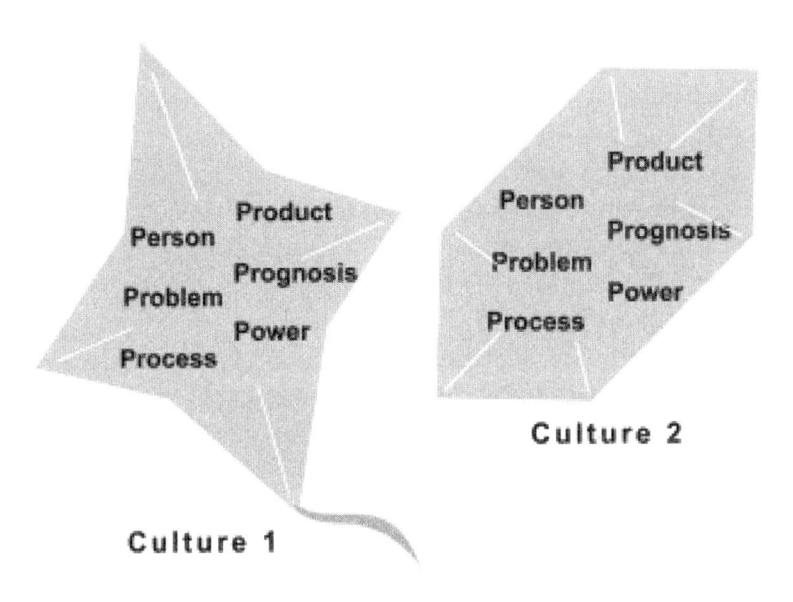

Diagram III.1 Culture and the 6 P's of Negotiation

The **Person** acts, negotiates and perceives according to his culture. In general, the **Process** or business model is very different from one culture to another. An American expects moderate investment rates in 4 years. An Asian expects a lower return on long term investment (20 years). A Latino expects high rates of return in the short term (less than a year), "How much am I making today?" Culture has an effect on the process.

Thanks to globalization, the quality of the **Product** is usually the same, regardless of its origin (where it was produced or assembled) or culture of the producer. If a visitor goes to Harvard University and wants to buy a souvenir (pens, t-shirts, etc.), he can see that most of these products come from other countries (Mexico, El Salvador, Jordan, etc.). Nonetheless, he is purchasing them at Harvard (U.S.A.).

There are exceptions where product differences occur due to cultural influence. For example, the "tortas ahogadas" (salsa coated sandwiches) of Guadalajara, a traditional product of that region in Mexico, are hard to find anywhere else.

The fourth P, **Power** depends on the culture, in the sense that different cultures use different sources of power. For example, the "intimidation of negotiation" is a source of power used in some cultures that does not work in others. Just the same, "humiliation" can be used as a source of power in some cultures. There are more manipulative cultures, and some are easier to convince than others. Not telling the whole truth or not presenting all the players are other forms that some cultures use more than others.

It's important to recall that power in a negotiation is, to a certain degree, the perception held by one party of the other. How does the other party see us? What impression do we give? These are the things that provide or take away power in a negotiation.

The 5th P, the **Problem**, also has cultural influence from the perspective that some cultures understand and separate the person from the problem, while others take every problem personally.

Finally, the 6th P, the **Prognosis**, depends on the culture and one's skill in analyzing the market information. The final message is that the negotiator that possesses a global vision of the negotiation will achieve high-yield, robust negotiations. The shortsighted negotiator whose focus is on "price" will clearly point the way towards failure. We can acquire this global vision by analyzing the negotiation in different dimensions and visualizing it within the framework of the 6 P's (**Person, Product, Process, Power, Problem** and **Prognosis**).

III.3 Global Vision of Negotiation

A global vision of the negotiation is the result of following the 10 P's of the methodology of sales and the 6 P's of negotiation. Diagram III.2 illustrates how the 10 P's of the methodology of sales are positioned in space and time with regard to the 6 P's of negotiation.

The first ones (10 P's), warn the salesman against continuing with bad opportunities and support him in selecting strategic accounts, identifying this way from very early on what process is worthwhile pursuing. The second set (6 P's), the main topic of **Deal**, invites us to make fewer mistakes and visualize multiple alternatives to the agreement and the strategies of negotiation.

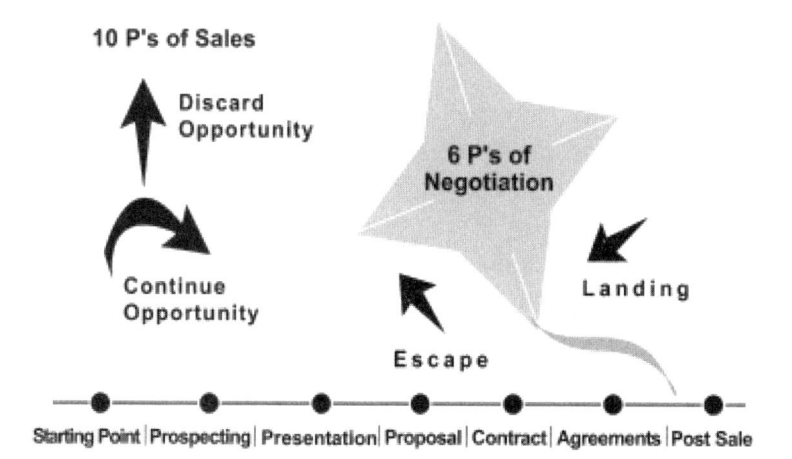

Diagram III.2 Global Vision of Negotiation in the Context of Business Development

III.4 The Key Differences between Cultures as the Driving Event of Negotiation.

Without Differences, There is No Need to Negotiate

Negotiating with different cultures is similar to negotiating with kids.

We will use this analogy of kids as a form of foreign culture. If you have children or have ever tried to reach a successful agreement with a child, you are familiar with the following situations:

After several attempts with your child to explain the benefits of coming to an agreement with you, you lose your patience, become exasperated and anger builds. This is what can result when negotiating with a culture different to yours. They simply don't get it.

You don't reach an agreement on good terms. Perhaps the pressure of time causes exasperation and makes you lose control, even to the point of yelling at your child.

The child is not listening to you, and you are not listening to him either. How many times does intolerance to that which is different cause us to fall into this situation?

You don't understand each other, as if you were speaking on different wavelengths or were coming from different planets. If you have conducted business with a foreigner, you may have asked yourself, "What is this person thinking?" You don't understand his reactions and don't know what to expect from the other party.

Your values, the child's and those of the person from a foreign culture are all different.

The perception of the value of things is as different for you as it is for the other person (different culture) and for the child. What may have value to us, may not have it to them. An example of this is the concept of "being on time."

The child's behavior, that of different cultures and yours, for example, are different when you are under the pressure of time.

The importance that the child or (culturally different person) assigns to making the right decision and the impact of the consequences are also very different from the importance that you may give to it.

At times we underestimate these things and don't believe we are being understood by the child or the different culture.

This is where we feel that the negotiator (adult) and the other party (the kid or different culture) are in two different worlds with very different degrees of importance and interests.

If a successful negotiation is a continuous dance of the interest of both parties with the objective of achieving maximum satisfaction (win-win), the big challenge is to satisfy the other party's interests, especially when they differ from yours.

Perhaps we are unable to identify with people because we are unfamiliar with them, but we believe that the other person's interests are similar to our own. With this mindset, we think that the other party thinks and acts exactly like we do. We believe that people act the same way in similar situations, which is routinely not the case.

Other similarities in negotiations with kids and with other cultures are:

Negotiations are complicated by the fact that we are negotiating with someone very different from us. We don't know what the other person's reaction will be. We don't understand what the most important thing is to the other party in the process of negotiation. When a child says he wants a toy and receives it as a gift but is unhappy, perhaps the child's real desire was for attention. In the same manner, of negotiations with the cultures of other countries, it will be important to know what factors are important.

The model by Dr. Jeswald Salacuse considers that there are 10 factors that affect the culture of negotiation. (Read about the 10 factors ahead.)

With kids, "the simple way" is the best form of communication, without many frills. Similarly with other cultures, we have to understand what is important to them. Be simple, quick and direct. Find the "no frills" way to arrive at the key point of the need of the other culture by asking what they are looking for: assurance, reliability or just price.

In summary, negotiating with other cultures is similar to negotiating with children in that it would appear that we are speaking different languages and are on different wavelengths.

The counterpart has different behaviors and attitudes on the same point. (To the adult, cost is very important. A kid may place little or no value on cost, as might another culture). Then, what is the most important point for the other party, if it is not price? Perhaps what is important is that we understand and satisfy him.

In another example, it's often important in an adult negotiation to know when and where to insist on the critical point of value to us, being cautious not to take it to an extreme and jeopardize the negotiation. With a kid or another culture, they may not perceive this as a risk and insist until they get what they want, without having any predetermined knowledge or fear of insisting too much.

Tolerance to things is different among cultures, children and adults. There are cultures with a higher tolerance towards others, and in general, adults are more tolerant than kids about certain things and circumstances. As a golden rule, he who is most tolerant is the best intercultural and intracultural negotiator.

On the other hand, just as we teach kids that for every action taken, there are positive or negative consequences, we see that also in negotiations with other cultures, we have to understand the consequences of each business decision. If, for example, we are speaking of a business culture, where there are not a lot of rules, we must be proactive, clear, and open about the consequences that would befall the parties if they break the agreement that has been reached.

Now, when we seek to reach an agreement with someone from our own culture, we know the typical behaviors. In the Mexican culture, a phone call confirming our next visit may be an indication of reaching an agreement to our prior negotiation. Contrast this behavior with the American, who usually requires a signed agreement as a symbol of commitment between the negotiating parties.

An example of the above occurred with a foreign client. For him, reaching an agreement simply meant a "Yes" over the phone without the need for anything in writing. It was expected that an additional business meeting was going to be scheduled by a phone call.

When the client did not hear from us, he assumed that the deal was canceled. In Mexico, it is generally not the custom for most people to confirm appointments. Reaching an agreement about the date of the next appointment suffices.

Different cultures see things in different ways. Their behaviors and attitudes toward others in specific situations differ greatly, depending on their own culture. Observing a great number of Mexicans, we found that there are important differences between the regions of Mexico. For example, in Mexico City, Guadalajara and Southern Mexico, the business culture is traditionally more formal and indirect than in the case of Monterrey and other cities in Northern Mexico. This doesn't mean that people from Mexico City act in a formal and indirect manner when they negotiate or that in Monterrey everyone is informal and direct in their negotiation style. These are preliminary research results and are not yet statistically validated. (Read more results in the Appendix).

How do we negotiate with other cultures? What are the steps to reach an agreement?

1. First, understand what they are looking for and what they really need.

2. Then, understand the details of the negotiation behavior of that culture (What is expected after the first visit, a follow up or closing? What's next?)

3. Understand how they buy and sell, who the decision makers are and who has influence over whom within the organization.

4. We must find out what solution we have or can generate to uniquely satisfy the needs of our clients in different cultures.

5. It is important to know why we've been selected, what our clients see in us and not in our competitors.

6. Know if we can meet the expectations of the other culture.

7. If, after an analysis, we know we can win this project and that it will be profitable, we must be sure that we can present it efficiently in a successful presentation or proposal to the client. (Here we must understand their protocol for receiving proposals and presentations. Do not just prepare them in the manner that you routinely make them). We must show added value and benefits to the client, instead of just displaying the characteristics of our products and services.

8. Tolerance towards other cultures and respect towards the customs of others are definitely the keys to success in this type of intercultural negotiation.

9. Letting the other culture speak first is another golden rule in negotiation.

10. Understand if our added value is something the other culture expects. Despite everything, we must be prepared in case we can't conduct business although we have invested time and resources. A business agreement may not happen on this occasion but we might use it as a platform for future transactions. It's important to understand this from the start, so we don't feel that we are working in vain.

11. In summary, we have to walk in the shoes of the other culture and understand what the other culture's perception and point of view would be concerning the actions, tactics and strategies of each phase of the process of negotiation.

In the research that I have conducted (read more about the results in the Appendix), I have found interesting trends in the Mexican business culture. Mexicans are shifting from the abuse of power to win-win negotiations. The new generation of businessmen tends to be of win-win negotiators, as opposed to traditional business negotiators who don't care about losing so long as the other party doesn't win. These traditional business negotiators must win every time.

According to Dr. Jeswald Salacuse, the factors that affect the culture of negotiation are the following, depending on the culture, whether it is a personal or a corporate culture.

1. Goal of the Negotiation (Contract or Relationship?)

Are we negotiating to specifically get a contract, or are we negotiating to develop a long-term relationship?

Mexico is a country traditionally based on interpersonal relationships and not only on contracts between the parties. Despite this be aware that there are groups in the country that prefer the contract to the relationship.

2. Attitude towards the Negotiation (Win/ Win or Win/ Lose)

In the win-win attitude, both parties seek to tie in their goals and negotiate until they achieve a mutual and integral benefit. This is in contrast to the other option, where one of the parties must concede on significant aspects to achieve the deal.

Based on a sample of more than 600 Mexican entrepreneurs, we note that the attitude of negotiation varies from the "over 55 year old" entrepreneurs (Win-Lose) to the young professional entrepreneurs (Win-Win). The explanation is that with the new trends and behaviors in business, you can no longer conduct negotiations where only one party wins. This is especially true where you are seeking long-term business relationships and repeat business. An indicator of this change is that there are less reported short-term clients. The current business trend is towards long-term repeat clients.

3. Personal Style (Informal or Formal?)

Formal negotiators usually address the participants by their titles and avoid getting involved in personal anecdotes. The informal negotiator seeks a friendlier, more personal relationship, trying to create a casual and comfortable environment for the negotiation.

Being informal in the negotiation is a style that has advantages and disadvantages, depending on the culture of the parties that are negotiating. On one hand, when being informal, things are easier, the ice is broken, there is empathy and we quickly get to the point. On the other hand, if our counterpart is more formal, he might be offended by our lack of formality. This could provoke a cultural clash that could delay the process of negotiation.

4. Communication (Direct or Indirect?)

Direct communication refers to the use of direct, simple and solid phrases to define situations. Indirect communication prefers to use "twists" or insinuations to express an opinion or a decision.

The direct negotiator expects a "yes" or "no" answer from the other party. It's common that there will be misunderstandings in the process of negotiation simply due to the type of communication. For example, if an indirect negotiator tells another, "Yes, I got the price, and we will come back next week to close the deal", perhaps the direct negotiator will infer that the deal has been closed, although nothing is closed yet. Since the direct negotiator is used to getting to the point, in this same example, the direct negotiator would say, "We haven't closed yet. We need another meeting with the client." It's important to understand if the other culture is more indirect in its communication than ours. This is why we should pay close attention to the way they negotiate. If we observe that this involves indirect communication, it would be good to confirm a "yes" or a "no" decision, so we always reach a conclusion, without offending the other party.

The indirect negotiator gives us false hope of being "in the running" as potential service providers. Then, when we least expect it, we get a cold bucket of water by not reaching an agreement in the negotiation we thought we had in our pocket. This is why I recommend considerable caution and not moving ahead when dealing with indirect people until we clearly understand the other party.

It's good to mention here that a direct negotiator might be perceived as being somewhat cold and calculating, to a degree, even rubbing us the wrong way. Despite this, we have to be tactful and very direct when we are negotiating with indirect negotiators, so as not to hurt their feelings.

Another cultural factor we have observed in negotiations between Mexicans and Americans is that a Mexican does not like us to tell him where he is wrong or what he's not doing right. Americans are usually the opposite. Mexicans don't like to make fun of their own weaknesses, while Americans often use self-deprecating humor. So, when we are face-to-face with persons from another culture, we must understand how direct or indirect we must be, using this to minimize the damage and friction between the negotiating parties and to achieve a win-win agreement.

5. Sensitivity to Time (High or Low?)

A high sensitivity to time reflects a strong adherence to punctuality and formality in the timing of decision-making and/ or compliance. Low sensitivity indicates, instead, more flexibility in changes of important dates and less punctuality in appointments, etc.

It's important to understand how the other culture negotiates. We should know beforehand if our counterpart is not punctual and if he has a low sensitivity to time. If he has a low sensitivity to time, we must be patient, tolerant and perhaps use the down time to conduct other activities, while we sit waiting in the reception area.

On the other hand, if we are not punctual, and we want to do business with cultures with a high sensitivity to time, beware! This might lead us to lose the business, since these cultures are intolerant of the lack of punctuality. Being late may be taken as a sign of disrespect or that we don't care about them. This is only one aspect of the sensitivity to time.

Another aspect is how quickly people reach an agreement. Some cultures take their time to reach an agreement, while others reach agreements rapidly.

6. Importance of Emotions (High or Low?)

Negotiators can show or hide their emotions. Some negotiators try to hide any feelings.

On the other hand, some have no qualms about emotionally voicing their answers or decisions.

Persons who demonstrate a high sensitivity to emotions are people who can easily establish empathy with others in the process of negotiation.

When initiating the first contact with the client, it's important to start as a high sensitivity person who will know how to reach the other. Be pleasant, and "break the ice." However, beware when it comes to the closing. It may require a person who is the complete opposite of you, with low sensitivity, who will not even show a smile on his face, like a good poker player who can mask his emotions.

There are cultures that show a higher sensitivity to emotions while negotiating. For example, after having reached an agreement with the other party, they will externalize this with phrases such as "yes" or "very well" and this can give the wrong perception to the other party, because it might be interpreted as "you fell for it" or "I won". This is why it is important to consider this when we are closing. We should not let doors that are about to close reopen, or we will not reach an agreement.

7. Format of Agreements (Specific or General?)

A specific format refers to the detailed wording of all the aspects relating to the **Deal**.

General contracts don't cover all the points and are intentionally left open to continue the relationship.

There are persons who negotiate the specifics and not the general terms and vice versa. If you enter into an agreement without reviewing the details, you are negotiating in a general way. If, on the contrary, you pay attention to all the details of the deal, you are definitely someone who negotiates specifics. There are no good or bad personal styles of negotiation. Every individual has his style, and we must respect and understand it to be able to reach a satisfactory agreement. If we know that the other party likes details, we should give him options along with the characteristics of each option. If on the contrary, we know that the other party is confused by options, let's keep our explanation simple and get right to the point.

8. Development of Agreements (Bottom-Up or Top-Down?)

There are styles that prefer to start the negotiation on general terms and on the way, address the specific issues. This is a style called "Top-down".

Others prefer to first define all the specific points of the deal and then leave the general context for the end. This style is "Bottom-up". This factor is directly related to what we reviewed in the format of agreement in factor number 7.

9. Learning about the Team's Organization Beforehand (Leader or Consensus?)

In some cultures, group decisions are taken absolutely by the leader, in an autocratic fashion. In others, there is a tendency for the team to find solutions and conclusions.

We should be aware that if there are several decision makers within our client's company, this will allow us to develop adequate strategies for each member of the team. It's recommended we learn about the way decisions are taken, if they are consensual or made by a single leader. This will make our efforts more efficient and secure a better closing.

10. Capacity for Risk Taking (High or Low?)

Negotiators with a high risk-taking capacity carry out business with a higher degree of uncertainty.

In contrast, those with a low-risk taking capacity seek to know all the details and avoid any complication that might arise before closing any deal.

If the counterpart is a high risk-taker, this will explain a lot of the actions of the process of negotiation. Knowing this ahead of time will allow us to negotiate more efficiently.

III.5 Strategy and Behaviors in International Negotiations

When we negotiate, our behavior is strategic, and these strategies may originate in our culture. We have personal background experiences that are reflected in our behavior when we negotiate, since we presume that others think like we do.

Furthermore, what the parties need and the order in which these needs are satisfied are elements that awaken our creative use of strategies.

In point 4, we saw how cultural factors affect the negotiation. Now let's analyze how these elements may translate into strategies that influence the type of behavior that the negotiator will apply. In the following chart III.1, we will discuss five strategies as they relate to typical behaviors in international negotiations.

Strategy	Behavior
Motivation	We find three types of behavior. First, the individual motivation, or personal interests. Second, the interest of others and last of all, the collective interests. Culture will affect the way we seek each one of these interests and will give us stereotypes of how the other party might behave.
Team Organization	Knowing if the other party will pursue the consensus of its members, or follow the leader, we can prepare ourselves to face this decision making process. Cultures that seek a consensus, generally focus more on personal relationships than the business at hand.
Form of Communication/ Information	This strategy may lead us to use a more direct or indirect approach as we say things, so that the other party does not feel culturally affected. The way that we present the information to the other party is a key element of this strategy.
Sensitivity to Time/ Priorities	We can have high or low sensitivity to time. Cultures with a high sensitivity value punctuality as well as speed in closing the deal. On the other extreme, we have cultures with a low sensitivity that place other values ahead of time. The importance of this behavior is that time can be one of the best elements to gain power in the negotiation.
Uncertainty	There are high risk cultures that have lived their entire history amidst unclear and highly uncertain scenarios. On the other hand we have cultures that are accustomed to low risk. This strategy shows us the way to prepare ourselves and present details, depending on the type of business, political and economic situations of both parties.

Chart III.1 Strategies and Behaviors in International Negotiations

We have tried to determine and analyze different strategies that clearly correspond to different behaviors that can be culturally influenced. In a certain way, we are trying to gain power in the negotiation with these different behaviors, that affect and influence our counterpart so that he can understand the way we do things.

In summary, we should recognize that every negotiator will use different strategies to achieve his objectives. His objectives in the negotiation are motivated by his needs. Our negotiations must be carried out with a clear vision of the value of time and priorities held by the other party.

Summary of Golden Rules while negotiating with another culture:

- Be tolerant
- Be polite
- Be respectful
- Be understanding
- Be patient
- Become a good listener
- Don't rush to conclusions

"Self-trust is the first secret of success." – Ralph Waldo Emerson

Chapter IV

When negotiating the sale of a product or service we have to be very creative due to global competitiveness. We don't have to be creative only when faced with multimillion dollar jobs, but also with very small deals. For instance, my kids enjoy selling my Spanish book editions at book fairs. For the fun of it, they have practiced the art of selling since a very early age. One of them, Habib, my 13 year-old and oldest of the four, is so good at selling that I know my methodology works not only with my clients, but also with my kids. At a particular Hispanic book fair, I recall a person approaching our stand and Habib asking her, "Do you speak Spanish?" The person did not. He didn't give up, but rather followed up by asking the same lady, "Does anyone in your family speak Spanish?" Her answer was again, "No." He persisted and asked her if she had a friend that spoke Spanish. She still responded, "No." His objective was to sell her a business book in Spanish, so he kept probing to find a buyer's motive. He finally asked her if she would like to speak Spanish, especially since the Hispanic population is growing without precedent in Texas and by year 2020 will reach approximately 60%, making solely English-speaking people a minority. This aroused her attention. Then he told her, "If you would like to tap into the Hispanic market in the States, maybe it would be a good idea to learn Spanish." Finally, she answered, "I would love to have the opportunity." Habib replied, "Here is a great business book in Spanish that will get you off to a good start." She bought the book. At subsequent events, he began making deals with neighboring vendors to buy our products if we drove business their way. Together with his siblings Emile, Antoine and Marcelle, he came up with the idea of raffling off one of the books for a dollar a ticket. They collected $45, increasing the effective sales price of that book by threefold.

Creativity is the key in sales and negotiations, and by helping our kids become better negotiators, we will create better communities.

Case Studies and Experiences of Negotiation

"Imagination is more important than knowledge." - Albert Einstein

This chapter contains the following topics:

IV.1 Chronicles of a Failed Negotiation

IV.2 A Negotiation that Exceeded Expectations

IV.3 A Negotiation is a Continuous Dance of Interests Behind Positions

IV.4 When the Big Ones Lose Power

IV.5 The Difference is in The "Closing Moment"

IV.6 Negotiating in Difficult Situations

IV.7 The Imbalance of Power and Win/Win Negotiations

IV.8 The Invisible Barriers of Negotiation

IV.9 Establishing the Standards of a Good Negotiation

IV.10 The Key is Preparing the Negotiation

IV.11 Negotiating with Difficult People

IV.12 Negotiation of a Perishable Product Past its Expiration Date

IV.1 Chronicles of a Failed Negotiation

The Purchase of Their Dream House

John and Mary were about to purchase their first house. Since they don't have children, they could choose any residential area that they liked. The ideal home, from their point of view, would be a two-bedroom house with a studio that they could use as an office.

After visiting many residential areas, they decided on a "green hill" zone. This was a new residential development that was heavily advertised in the local newspaper. In fact, they noticed in the real estate section that there were promotions for first buyers in this development. Homes were selling in the $210,000 to $300,000 range.

Before visiting the model home, John called Dorothy, the sales manager of the developer of the "green hill" zone. Dorothy told John that if they visited the home in the afternoon, they would be meeting with her. In the morning, she explained, the salesman was a new man, David, who could not take care of them as she would.

Since John had a lot of experience in negotiating, he ignored Dorothy's suggestion and met with David the following morning. A $15,000 discount promotion was running, available to anyone who decided to purchase a house that had already been built.

When John arrived, he asked David to show him the houses that had the $15,000 dollar discount. David showed him homes that prior to any discount, were in the price range of $210,000 to $280,000. John and Mary decided on a home that cost $210,000. Subtracting the $15,000 promotion that David offered, the price of the house would come to $195,000.

John, after spending all morning with David, comments, "I am interested in the house but in 8 months, could you reserve an identical one for me at the price of $195,000?" David replied, "No problem. In fact, Dorothy wants to talk to you if you have time. She'll be here in just a moment." To this John replied, "Oh, no thanks. We have to leave right now, but we'll be back later. By the way, do you think that's the best price, or could Dorothy give us an extra discount?" David, who was inexperienced and didn't realize that he had conceded a lot without having secured the client's interest to purchase replied, "I think it's likely that she can reduce it, though not a lot."

John and Mary went for a ride and came back an hour later, near closing time to meet Dorothy. Dorothy told them that she was very upset with David, because he made a mistake and said things that he shouldn't have. John tells Dorothy, "Don't worry, Dorothy. We're going to buy the house. We just need to fine-tune the price. If I paid you right now, what would be your best price?" Dorothy answers, "You already have my best price." To which John replies, "Look Dorothy, my wife and I have already invested a whole day in this lovely development, and we are interested. I insist you give me your best offer so we can close the deal."

Dorothy says, "I am going to talk to my general manager, Gregory, but I doubt very much he'll give us an extra discount." Dorothy calls Gregory, and Gregory won't concede anything more, not a cent.

John loses his patience and says, "Let me talk to your boss. I'm sure he won't lose the sale. The economy is in a slump, unemployment is high and you are putting on airs. Let's see. Put me through to Gregory, and I'll explain the situation to him." Dorothy tried unsuccessfully to locate Gregory and seeing that they couldn't reach an agreement, finally broke into tears.

What happened? Where did the negotiation fail? 1) The inexperienced salesman conceded too much, too soon. 2) He conceded without getting the client to commit, exhausting his range of discounts too quickly. The buyer felt that if from the start he got a discount of $15,000, by the closing he should have gotten at least another $8,000. This negotiation got off to a bad start, and the buyer thought that best thing was not to reach an agreement. If the buyer had made the purchase, he would always wonder if he might have gotten a bigger concession. Since the first $15,000 discount was obtained so quickly, its value was diminished and appeared to simply be the product of marketing. On the other hand, if the salesman had sold the house below the acceptable range of discount, he would have felt that he had not made a profitable sale. Thus, the bad start of this negotiation took us to negative results for all the parties and in this case, the best alternative was not to have a deal.

In a negotiation, both parts have to come out winning, even if in perception only.

If we analyze this case with the P's of negotiation, the negotiation bogged down in the **Process**. The wrong game was played from the start of the negotiation. It's also important to observe the **Persons**. If Dorothy had come in from the start, the negotiation might have taken another path. With the **Product**, the sudden discount created a **Problem** which overshadowed the **Price** and brought about a negative result. The **Power** of experience helped John in the beginning in dealing with David and contributed to the false **Prognosis** of success.

IV.2 A Negotiation that Exceeded Expectations

Peter took his mother-in-law Alice to the Los Angeles International Airport. She had been visiting him and his wife Martha for more than 2 months. Alice had an expired plane ticket to Houston. Peter had considered his options before arriving at the Los Angeles Airport. His options were: 1) to call the airline and tell the person in charge about the changes, probably incurring a fee or 2) to address the situation upon arrival at the airport. The consequences of delaying the negotiation, in the worst case scenario, were that the flight would be full and Alice would stay a few more days. On the positive side, if he negotiated face-to-face, maybe he could get them to not charge a fee because of the expiration of the airplane ticket.

Peter chose to leave the ticket as it was and solve the **Problem** in **Person** at the airport despite the risk of his mother-in-law having to fly at a later date.

Upon arrival at the Los Angeles Airport, Peter went to the check-in counter and observed the situation in progress. People were hysterical, and there was a long waiting list. It was complete chaos - so bad that one upset passenger was yelling at Josephine, the young attendant checking in the passengers.

Peter, a good negotiator, carefully observed this, noting in great detail everything in the environment and with a good tone of empathy approached Josephine. "You have so much patience with all these nasty people. If I was in your shoes, I don't know what I'd do," Peter told Josephine. "You're right. You know, it's like this every day, especially during this season. It's nice to have passengers like yourself who understand the situation we are in," Josephine said. "Well, you know what it's like to have your mother-in-law in the house visiting for several months?" Peter asked. To that Josephine replied, "It must be nice to please your wife." "That it is," Peter replied and added,

"Look, Josephine, could you please check and see if there's a possibility of sending my mother-in-law home in First Class? It would make this visit to Los Angeles a memorable one and she would be happy right up to the end of her visit. This way, next time she'll be happy to return." Josephine replied, "I would be so happy if my husband treated my mother like that. Let me see if we have room." Finally, Josephine did find a seat in First Class, and Peter got Alice the change of her expired return ticket without the penalty.

Moral of the story:

1) Prepare yourself before negotiating any issue,
2) Establish empathy towards the other party,
3) Put yourself in the other person's shoes,
4) Study the situation and the context of the negotiation,
5) Analyze and perceive how the environment can benefit the negotiation,
6) Do not be afraid to ask for anything,
7) Be sure of yourself,
8) Don't mention your weak points (To "I have an expired ticket. How can you help me?" the answer would probably be, "This is not a charity, Sir. It's an airline."),
9) Do not give extra information, unless it is requested.

Prepare: In this case, Peter analyzed things and decided to risk changing his mother-in-law's ticket at the airport. He considered the alternatives of not reaching an agreement. The worst case scenario was sending Alice home on another day and paying the additional charges. We recommend that in your projects or everyday negotiations, you evaluate your alternatives before blindly "throwing yourself into a negotiation."

Develop Empathy: Peter broached the **Problem** of the moment with the airline employee, putting aside the **Problem** of the expired ticket. After putting himself in Josephine's shoes and understanding the frustrating situation she was experiencing, Peter had the ability to move Josephine by presenting a situation that would be very empathetic. Based on Josephine's reply, Peter continued developing this momentary relationship with her and finally exceeded the expectations of the negotiation.

Study the situation: Before asking for an upgrade to First Class, Peter made Josephine feel that the person who was traveling was her own mother.

Perceive the context of the negotiation: Peter wondered how he'd feel if he were Josephine, with an airport full of hysterical people and chaos everywhere. He used this to establish empathy from the start.

Don't be afraid to request or offer: If you seem afraid and don't ask, believe me, you'll get nothing in return. It's commonly said that "if you don't speak up, God will not hear you." How many times do you leave a negotiation thinking, "Darn it! I should've given them the 10% discount and they would've taken it. But I gave them 20%," or "What a disaster! I paid $50 without even offering a lower amount!" Don't leave value on the negotiating table. Neither party will benefit from that.

Don't provide additional information: If Peter had mentioned from the start that he had an expired ticket, the best thing he would have obtained would have been to not pay the difference. Nonetheless, he obtained much more.
Here we've analyzed the

- **Person**: Peter and Josephine,
- **Problem**: the expired airline ticket,
- **Process**: how the steps of the negotiation were carried out,
- **Prognosis**: that exceeded expectations thanks to the planning of the negotiation, where we have to set our sights on the highest point so we arrive where we want to, and last of all,
- **Power**: in Peter's negotiation, it increased as Josephine began developing the perception of Peter as a coherent, understanding, objective man, who supports his mother-in-law.

This case is only used for illustration purposes. The author doesn't encourage the readers to be manipulative in similar situations.

IV.3 A Negotiation is a Continuous Dance of Interests Behind Positions

John was boarding a plane at Los Angeles International Airport, bound for Mexico City.

As he boards the plane and takes his seat, he notices that seat 1A in the first row, which was assigned to him, has more space that allows you to easily stretch your legs. To his surprise, John meets his best friend, Peter, who is traveling in the fifth row of the plane, sitting next to an American, Tom. It's uncomfortable for some people to ask strangers to change their seats, and, above all, when they belong to a different culture, there is an additional barrier in the negotiation, the cultural barrier. John asks himself how he can ask Tom to change seats with him, and John, as a good negotiator, looks for an advantage he can offer, trying to find "something" that will benefit them both. John decides that he is willing to give up his premium seat in order to sit next to Peter.

Tom is a tall man and doesn't fit too comfortably in the seat he has been assigned. Observing this, John addresses Tom with, "Dear sir, would you mind changing your seat for mine? You'd have more room to stretch your legs, and I would get to sit with my best friend who I see is seated here next to you." Tom replies, "My pleasure, and thanks for thinking of my comfort. I always ask for the first seat, and I was just thinking about that."

John is seated in a window seat and Peter in an aisle seat. Among other things, John asks Peter, "How important on a plane is the seat you are in?" John replies, "You know, the only thing I am interested in is being able to run out of the plane so I can make it on time to my appointments or make my connecting flight. I always ask for the aisle seat and it doesn't matter whether it's Coach or First Class. Sitting in the aisle gives me the flexibility to move without bothering the person next to me."

Peter replies, "How interesting! On the contrary, I love to enjoy the scenery, take my time, and relax, which is why I always ask for the window seat." John asks, "What are we waiting for? Let's change seats!"

This case illustrates the differences between positions and interests in negotiation. Dr. Roger Fisher and Dr. William Ury state,"If you negotiate interests, you increase business for the parties. If you negotiate positions, it is likely that profit will be left on the negotiating table, and no one will take it."

In this case, the position is the seat number, the row number, First Class or Coach, or window or aisle seat. The interest is the reason behind the position. Why do we want First Class? Why the window or aisle? Maybe the reason is to enjoy the scenery, to run out to catch a connection, to hang your suits so they don't wrinkle, or to support an interest of belonging, safety or nostalgia. The interest is the need we are satisfying behind the position of price, the seat number, time, reach, etc.

If we know someone is interested in flying First Class (position), we should ask ourselves what the interest really is. If his interest or reason is a better meal but the food in First Class is similar to Coach, then the interest of flying First Class will not be achieved. If the interest in flying First Class is only to have suits or dresses hanging in the front section so they don't wrinkle, I can assure you that the satisfaction of this interest will not matter if you are sitting in First Class or not. Understanding the reason behind a position of negotiation may invite us to offer creative solutions that satisfy the interest of the parties without compromising positions.

In literature, the classic example of negotiation that scholars use is that of the two oranges as a further illustration of the above case study.

With this example, we can numerically prove that negotiation is continuous problem solving, satisfying interests and not positions.

Two persons are negotiating to divide twenty oranges among themselves. The traditional mentality dictates that half the oranges for each one is the win/win solution, this is, 10 oranges for each party in the negotiation. The number of oranges is the position, and the traditional negotiation is a negotiation of positions. If they enter into the competitive process of give and take, perhaps the smartest one will keep 15 and the other one the rest. Well, this is not a win/win negotiation. The win/win negotiation occurs if both of them are aware of the interests behind the position of quantity and ask, "Why does each one want 10 oranges, why do they want the oranges at all, or what are they going to do with them?"

If one of the two wants the oranges to make juice and the other wants them as an ingredient to make a cake, the negotiation of interests has better results, since the person who wants to make the juice might end up keeping 100% of the liquid and the person who wants to make a cake can take 100% of the peel. This way, they both obtain more than if they only received 50% of the total number of oranges.

The **Problem** that comes into play is cultural. If we are open and disclose the interest behind the position, as in this case of the oranges, and if we are the one who wants the oranges to make a cake, and we know the other party is interested in the juice, believe me, we will try to "milk" that and sell the juice at a higher price, while manipulating the situation to make the other party believe that the peel is garbage and of no use to us. We will be doing him a favor by disposing of it, though we know that this is what we are most interested in.

How should things really be? Let's be honest and open up, bit by bit, as the business relationship with the other party develops. In real life, not everything is a rose garden, so we need part of the liquid, part of the peel and maybe some of the orange seeds. Then the key is to know what we need of the three things and importantly, also know what the other party is most interested in and with this make a list of priorities and design a strategy of concessions in the negotiation.

The moral is that even if the negotiation of interests increases the "booty" for the parties, we have to consider the possible abuse of power before opening up completely and showing our true interests. Develop a good working relationship and discover the interests and priorities of the other party so we can design the strategy and sequence of concessions.

I've provided the example of oranges because the position elements of negotiation become clear to the reader. Now we can return to airplane example and analyze the:

- **Person**: John, Tom, Peter,
- **Problem**: the plane seats,
- **Process**: how the steps of the negotiation occurred and how to be open to negotiate interests,
- **Prognosis**: that exceeded the expectations, thanks to the planning of the negotiation, understanding why the other party might benefit in exchanging plane seats with me and,
- **Power**: of negotiation in understanding the interest behind the position, using it in favor of a win/win negotiation, and not using it to manipulate the negotiation.

IV.4 When the Big Ones Lose Power

Imagine the following situation: You belong to a small firm and have just invented a new product. This product needs to be associated with a large firm that has an established name in the market in order to introduce the product to the market faster.

The power of negotiation stems not from ourselves, but rather from how the other party perceives us. A small player can maintain a level of power when negotiating with a larger party with the following strategy:

 Continuously reminding the big party that despite his size, he does not have the particular specialty you possess, which is why you will be positioning him in areas of opportunity he did not participate in. You are supporting him, so he can diversify.

Sometimes the errors of the big party are paid by the small firm. Differing from most of the large firms where paperwork and "bureaucracy" get lost in the process, in small firms, in their effort to excel and grow, they find their decision making process is more agile than large firms. Due to this bureaucracy, many times the product of the small firm pays the consequences by not being taken into account or rotated adequately, because it gets lost next to the other products of the large firm. Thanks to its reputation, the large one can cover its mistakes and take the luxury of billing them to the small firm.

We conclude that the small firms that are familiar with these situations and foresee them can increase their power of negotiation.

Despite everything, the firm that has the know-how must assign itself the value it deserves and define this way its market value.

The typical tendency in a negotiation is for the big guy to intimidate the small one, which is why he gives in or makes ample concessions to the degree of losing business in the process of positioning his business.

In this case, the **Process** of negotiation is more important than the **Persons** or the **Product** to negotiate and it is of vital importance to put in place a clear strategy of pre-negotiation (before entering the **Process**).

It's important to have a long-term vision in place in a contractual document between the parties, stating what is acceptable and unacceptable in the business relationship.

The worst thing a small firm can do is let itself become intimidated by the large firm and devaluate its market share.

Everyone has a value. **KNOW HOW TO SELL YOURSELF WELL.**

We have observed this same tendency in negotiations between a Mexican and an American. When a Mexican is negotiating with another Mexican in the United States, he does so in a very competitive fashion. When an Anglo Saxon enters the negotiation, the Mexican is intimidated and becomes "smaller in stature", lowering his guard. This is not a general situation, though it has been observed in a large number of negotiations between Mexicans and Americans. Sometimes the Mexican will scuttle the negotiation as a perceived way to achieve equality.

We repeat, if you do not give yourself the value you deserve, no one will give it to you. Do not be intimidated by the presence of a larger player. I ask, "Who is the large one?" This is only a perception.

On the other hand, we have the Latino with a lot of power who treats his counterpart arrogantly, taking advantage of the situation. Let's recall that grandeur is not measured by the "abuse" of power, but by the "use" of power to obtain a win/win negotiation for the parties. We recall David and Goliath. Surprise the larger player with strategies, just as David surprised Goliath. Build alliances and coalitions with other small players, this way, you change the framework of the negotiation to increase your power.

Remember that there are many more small and medium sized firms, and that they are the driving force of the economies of our countries.

Shift the power in the negotiation. It's in your hands.

Here we analyze the:

- **Person**: small and large firms,
- **Problem**: the imbalance of power of the large one,
- **Process**: changing the framework of action to increase your power of negotiation,
- **Prognosis**: that exceeded expectations thanks to the pre-planning of the negotiation,
- **Product**: a new product in a competitive market and
- **Power**: the perception the large firm has of the small one and vice versa.

IV.5 The Difference is in The "Closing Moment"

The "moment of closing" is a small window in time where the client decides to "close" with us and the only thing pending on our part is "reaffirming" that he has made the correct decision.

This window in time opens and closes quickly. The successful negotiator has the sensitivity to know when the client is at the "moment of closing" and must not let him escape. The client typically invents objections at the "moment of closing" to reaffirm and justify his decision to close with us. If we don't know how to deal with these final objections, we may not close, even though the client wants a closing.

To close efficiently, we must know how to identify when we are at the "moment of closing", and both parties must keep a "closing mentality."

The phase of prospecting clients is where the main objective is to open all the possible windows of opportunity. When we reach the phase of closing and more specifically the "moment of closing", we must not leave open or semi-open any windows of the multiple kind that open and close in the market of opportunity. All windows and doors must be tightly shut so the closing is sealed.

There might be multiple moments of closing in a negotiation. The key is to close each moment tightly without attaching it to the next one.

Among the factors that affect these moments of closing we have:

> 1) The process of negotiation (**Process**),
> 2) The plan of negotiation (strategies, options, alternatives, etc.),
> 3) The negotiator (**Person**),
> 4) The needs of the parties,
> 5) The perceived value of what is being sold (**Power**),
> 6) The culture, etc.,
> 7) Knowing the product well (**Product**).

If one of the parties does not have a "closing mentality", even though we prepare ourselves and have the most creative strategies of negotiation, we will not achieve an efficient closing.

When we want to close and we have done our homework to design a plan of negotiation for a specific business situation, it's almost sure we will close. This condition cannot occur only on one side of the negotiating table, both parties must have a "closing mentality."

If the counterpart does not have a "closing mentality", we should re-evaluate if we are with the appropriate **Person**, that is, the "decision maker".

Understand the situation and question if it is really worthwhile pursuing this **Process** of negotiation. Perhaps the client is only evaluating options and is communicating that indirectly, but we perceive that he doesn't have a "closing mentality".

The characteristics of a negotiator with a "closing mentality" are, he:

1) Knows what he wants,
2) Knows what he and the other party need,
3) Does not abandon the road to closing,
4) Avoids surprises,
5) Avoids any detour from the objective ("The closing"),
6) Carries out creative actions to achieve the closing.

To achieve a "closing mentality", among other things, you need to:

1) Plan every movement and action on the way to the negotiation,
2) Prepare information on the client, the market, his products and services and competition,
3) Think creatively,
4) Think objectively,
5) Forget your egocentrism and selfishness,
6) Control your feelings and reactions,
7) Be proactive,
8) Be honest,
9) Think "closing".

Finally, to close efficiently in the "moment of closing", we need to do two things: remember we are already there and maintain our "closing mentality".

Here is an actual case of a very successful consulting services salesman that I'd like to share with you.

One fine day, the phone in Joe's office rings. He is a salesman of services of the firm "Consulting", located in the southern region of Mexico. The phone call is from Miriam, an executive of "W", located in northern Mexico. Miriam is requesting a proposal from Joe, because she has learned about the services of "Consulting" through the Internet.

Miriam is getting quotes from two other consulting firms with which "W" had previous work experience. They are all located in the North. The exception is "Consulting". From the start, "Consulting" had a losing hand, since it was not known by any action, just through the Internet. Furthermore, its offices were not located near the client.

She makes her request to Joe in the following manner: "Look, Joe, we need a proposal for 100 work hours of your consulting services. We are contacting you because we learned about your consulting services through your web page." Joe responded, "That's fine, Miriam. Before making a proposal though, I'd like to know more about the needs of your firm. Maybe you don't need 100 hours of consulting services. Maybe you need less. Can I talk to the person within 'W' who has the need for consulting?" Miriam replied, "The user? That is an excellent idea. You may be right. Why don't you contact Margaret, who can give you that information, then send us your best proposal?" Margaret was ahead of him and called first, saying, "Hi, Joe. It's Margaret from the firm 'W.' I believe Miriam spoke to you about our needs. We have to have a proposal from you as soon as possible." Joe answered, "Sure, Margaret. In fact, you beat me to it. I was just about to call you. I'd like to know exactly what it is you need from my firm before I prepare a proposal."

Well, after the long and detailed explanation from Margaret, Joe proposed that he could really perform their diagnosis in two hours for a specific fee, and if he got the job, he would credit the time spent for the diagnosis.

The moment of closing was defined. The client was about to make a decision to acquire the consulting services. What was not clear was whether it would be from "Consulting" or from the competition.

It's at this "moment of closing" when we must exercise a persistent "closing mentality", where we must not leave any door half open. Every single one must be closed.

Joe had made Margaret such an attractive proposal that she could not turn it down, if she was really interested in his services. Nonetheless, for some reason, Joe senses that something is wrong, because the intensity of calls from Margaret have cooled down. On the last call from Margaret, she says, "You know, Joe, I think your proposal is too good and thinking it over, we'd like to leave it for when we can do things as we should. Let's think about doing this diagnosis next year." Once the conversation between Joe and Margaret was over, Joe called Miriam, with whom there was already a certain air of empathy and who had been Joe's initial contact.

Joe asked Miriam, "Hey, Miriam, I am surprised that with a proposal as attractive as I made you, you are not considering it for this year. Is there any other reason you are not moving forward with it?" Miriam told Joe, "It's really because they don't know who you are as a vendor of services yet. Margaret's reputation within the firm is at stake if things don't turn out well and she doesn't use one of the other suppliers we have already worked with." Then Joe replied, "What would you think if I make Margaret an offer that, to minimize her concern on this occasion, I will put our consulting fees at risk if her expectations are not met. You won't have to pay us anything except travel expenses. We are so sure of our services that we can risk that." Miriam said, "Hey, I think that's fabulous. Why don't you call Margaret?" Joe calls Margaret right away and tells her, "Look, Margaret, could it be that maybe you are concerned because you have never seen our services in action? What do you think if we offer to risk our fees if we don't cover your expectations? You don't pay us anything except our travel expenses. This way, I can prove to you that we are sure of what we do, because I am guaranteeing it." At that moment Margaret told Joe, "Well, I think that's great. Let me talk it over with my boss", and Joe replies, "Very well. I'll wait on the line. Go find your boss". Margaret locates her boss and gets back on the line with Joe, literally saying, "O.K. Joe. You've closed every door and cornered me. It's a **Deal**. We'll start on the work next week."

The moral is that Joe not only noticed that it was the "moment of closing", but also exercised a "closing mentality".

Once again we'll analyze from the 6 P's of **negotiation** the relevant ones to the above case, to be able to observe the ones where the bottleneck occurred, which in this case were the

- **Person**: the lack of confidence in a service provider was the greatest barrier to a non-agreement,
- **Product:** the consulting was good. All that was missing was to inspire trust in the client,
- **Process**: it was important to take into account the sequence of the negotiation as well as the approved order in the process of communication,
- **Power**: the perception that existed of the different decision makers,
- **Prognosis**: Because we were convinced of the value of our services, we could transmit this to the client and thus, predict a good **Deal**.

IV.6 Negotiating in Difficult Situations

Case Study of the Mall

Imagine the following situation: You are with your family on a Sunday stroll through the mall with your five children and your wife.

For some reason that weekend, the parking lot of the mall was full to bursting, and finding a parking spot took an average of 45 minutes to an hour of waiting.

After you have waited in an orderly fashion for 35 minutes, staying in line behind a trail of cars in the parking lot, you notice that a car starts to back up. You start up the motor of your van to get into the space the other car is about to leave. Nonetheless, a car with 3 football players inside comes from the opposite direction and also tries to park in the same space that was just left empty.

You have several options to choose from at that moment: 1) Ignore the football players and maybe get lucky, if they leave soon. 2) React and maybe wind up in a brawl, three to one, besides looking like a fool in front of your family, 3) Surprise the football players with some tactic.

What you finally decided to do was ask the person at the wheel to toss a coin for it. Since neither one of you knew how long the other one had been waiting, it was probably fair to let a third party act as a judge. Since there were no witnesses, the best alternative was to flip a coin for the space.

Since this case occurred in the United States, where there generally is a sense of what's fair and what's not, the players were surprised, but thought the alternative of the coin toss was a good one. This might not have worked in another country in this precise manner.

Let's go over the steps to follow when dealing with a difficult person:

First, negotiate with ourselves, controlling our emotions and reactions.

Understand the other party. Try to listen to the counterpart as much as possible.

Ignore and Surprise are two of the most famous tactics used to confront difficult people and are recommended by experts on the subject, such as William Ury.

Case Study of the Airplane

Another case where we found a difficult situation began when John was on the way home on a flight he took every Friday afternoon. This time, John had forgotten to get a souvenir for his kids, but he realized this only while on the flight.

Reacting quickly, as the flight attendant went down the aisle of the plane offering candy to the passengers, John asked her, "Madam, would you be so kind as to give me 5 candy bars for my kids?" In a loud, sarcastic voice the flight attendant told John, "Are your children also on the plane?" "Yes", he replied, "They are in my mind and in my heart."
The flight attendant was surprised by John's answer, since she had expected an equally sarcastic comeback to her comment. He could've said, "Yes. You don't see them, but I do." And then further to that, "Do you think if they were with me, I'd be asking you for candy?"

It's so easy to reply with sarcasm and thus, not achieve the final objective of the negotiation. In this case, since the flight attendant was "agreeably" surprised, her answer to John was, "It's sweet that you think of your children that way. I am not only giving you 5 candy bars, but take two to each one."

What is the moral of the story? We will always come across drastic situations with difficult, sneering, "radioactive" people. What to do? Definitely, don't attack. Catch them off guard, "pull the rug out from under them". Surprise them!

Case Study of the Purchase of Computer Equipment

Another case of a difficult situation is the sale of a hundred computer systems by the firm "CORP" to its client, "CLIENT".

The plot unfolds after the sale of the computer equipment by the firm "CORP" to its client "CLIENT" has been made. Joe was the "CORP" salesman and Robert was the "CLIENT" purchaser. A day after the merchandise had been delivered, Robert urgently tried to locate Joe at his corporate office. Robert did not find Joe, because after making this big sale, he had decided to take a long vacation.

Robert did not wait for Joe to return from his vacation and tried to communicate with Joe's boss. He couldn't do that, and he finally reaches the person in charge of customer service for "CORP", Peter.

Peter asks Robert during their telephone conversation, "What can we do to help you? We hope the hundred computers are functioning properly, and if not, we are here to help you."

Robert was furious and started the conversation yelling, "What can you do to help me? I ask myself the same thing. You and your whole organization are all corrupt, good-for-nothings. You sell lies and do not deliver what you promise. What is the point of talking to customer service? I want to talk to the "top guy" in your organization. I'm going to return the whole lot of trash that your equipment is."

"Mr. Robert, please tell me how we failed you as a firm. What is the problem? Believe me, whatever the problem is, we are going to find a solution." To this Robert replied, "You are all just trained to talk pretty, but when it comes to solving problems, I don't think you know what to do."

Peter replied, "Let's talk, please. What is upsetting you? C'mon, tell me, what is your real problem? What's more, if you'd like I can visit you at your offices at this very moment, and we can discuss this in person in detail. We will solve your problem, no matter what it is. I just want to know what it was that we did wrong and what the damage is. Give us an opportunity to first understand what the problem is."

To this, Robert replies, "O.K., O.K., O.K., it seems like the least you guys can do. Come to my office and understand our problem. I will expect you in half an hour."

If we observe what has been happening up to this moment, Peter has gained ground and prepared the scenario of negotiation. Robert is not as angry anymore or reactive as in the beginning of the conversation. By having a recess, things cool down and the anger decreases. Besides, all Peter has done up to now has been listening to Robert and not counterattacking or contradicting him. On the contrary, Peter has followed, up to this moment, the steps the experts recommend: 1) listen to the other party, 2) let him vent, 3) understand what is upsetting him, 4) don't react against him and 5) control our emotions of anger or frustration that stem from being offended by the other party.

Let's see what happens at Robert's office. When Peter arrives at Robert's offices, he is met immediately, since the problem was very important to the firm "CLIENT".

Robert, with a different attitude, greets Peter and says, "I am grateful that you have taken the time to come all the way out to our offices. That gives me a good indication that we will solve this problem. You see, the problem is that the computers that you have sold us are brand 'C' and all of the internal components are from other brands, 'v', 'w' and 'g'. We are very concerned that when our clients receive them in a few days, they are going to complain about this situation. This order was a sure sale and is the most important sales quota of the year. It's very important to the survival of the firm."

Peter replies "Mr. Robert, if that is the problem, we have two solutions, Number one is to offer you the reference of the clients of your clients who have been using these 'C' computers with 'v','w', and 'g' components. It's just that, due to globalization, there are no longer products from a single brand, but rather a mix of brands. That is the standard of the industry and you could prove that to your client."

"Option 2 is to make a special order from computer manufacturer 'C' that only includes 'C' components, only that would have to be a special order and would cost more."

To this Robert replies, "Ah, this is very surprising to me. I was unaware that this is the standard of the industry. My, my, things do change. Well, in that case, I don't think a special order is justified. Thank you for your support. Like I've said before, this firm "CORP" has always helped us out in a bind."

As you see, once again the key is to surprise the client and not react to his insults or anger. Like Peter, we must not let our emotions get the best of us. When the client offends you, try to imagine that he is praising you. Let him vent. Once the part of the person is solved, start to work on solving the problem. Once again we analyze the 6 P's of negotiation to observe where the bottleneck is. In this case it was the

- **Person**: difficult people,
- **Product***:* the computer systems,
- **Problem**: the computers were assembled with parts from different suppliers,
- **Process**: it was important to first address the problem of the person and then the product,
- **Power**: the perception of the client who feels let down when he doesn't get what he "thought" he was buying. In this case there was a lack of communication and,
- **Prognosis**: the total satisfaction of the client without regrets.

IV.7 The Imbalance of Power and Win/Win Negotiations

Win/win negotiations are more successful in the long term but are harder to obtain. To reach a win/win negotiation, both parties have to concede a little. Both parties must understand what's behind the position of the other party.

In theory it's pretty easy, but when you carry it out, it gets complicated. How do you reach a win/win negotiation, especially when in a negotiation of two parties, there is an imbalance of power?

How do we balance power? After understanding the factors that affect the negotiation for each of the parties, we have to put each party's power on a scale and analyze what is making our negotiation successful or not.

What provides power in a negotiation? Among other things:

- Information,
- Perception,
- Standards,
- References,
- Precedents,
- Relationships.

The real power is the one that sees in its power the opportunity of reaching a win-win negotiation with the other party.

How can we tell who has the power in their favor in a negotiation?

- By listening,
- By analyzing,
- By understanding the process of negotiation.

How do we reduce the power of the other or shift power to our side of the negotiating table?

- Preparing ourselves with tactics, concepts and negotiation skills.

The key is in the balance of power and in the perception of the same.

Balance of Power = $P_{a1} - P_{b1} + P_{a2} - P_{b2}$
P_{a1} = Power of person a in point 1 of negotiation
P_{a2} = Power of person a in point 2 of negotiation
P_{b1} = Power of person b in point 1 of negotiation
P_{b2} = Power of person b in point 2 of negotiation

Let's consider, for a moment, the role of a third party who functions as a mediator. This role is important, since the third party will objectively analyze who has more power and how to use this power to conduct a win-win negotiation.

At the end of the day, negotiation is a "give and take" between the parties to reach an agreement. This "give and take" could seem more efficient if we consider a third party. We negotiate as "You" and "I", but thinking of or using a third "He" gives us an opportunity to objectively observe both parties and analyze the power of each.

Let's imagine that we are negotiating the purchase/sale of pencils. The pencil salesman has a sales plan to sell 100,000 pencils during the year. It's the end of the year, and he has 3000 pencils left to cover his plan. On the other hand, the pencil purchaser needs 5000 pencils, and the price he needs is 10% below the price offered to him by the salesman.

If the purchaser knows about the needs of the salesman in reaching his sales plan, he has more power over the salesman. If the salesman knows that the purchaser needs 5000 pencils within a month because they are going to give them to their clients for Christmas, this will also give the salesman certain power over the purchaser.

A third person might be able to obtain this information more readily from the parties and propose a win-win solution.

IV.8 The Invisible Barriers of Negotiation

Simple and complex negotiations have something in common, the barriers of negotiation.

These barriers are layers of resistance we have to avoid or deal with to reach a win-win negotiation.

A barrier is a hurdle we have to overcome. Think about how we can remove the ones we'll find, or plan strategies to knock down the barriers in the process.

The key is in brainstorming to detect the types of barriers that we might face in the process of negotiation before entering it. Once we have identified them, we must understand what type of barriers they are. These can be personal, process, cultural or even natural barriers. As in math, when we have a complex problem, some good advice is to divide it in several segments and solve it step by step, without losing sight of the whole equation.

Personal barriers have to do with the interrelationship between the persons negotiating, "the chemistry", people and difficult situations, talents and skills of the parties, the number of people participating in the negotiation, and others.

The process barriers deal with the type of organization with which we are negotiating, some being more bureaucratic than others. Some might be family firms. Others may be international corporations.

Cultural barriers have to do with the cultural differences of the participants, (business culture, country, etc.).

Natural barriers are those inherent to the projects in question or the issue that is being negotiated, for example, established prices or industry standards.

As an illustration, if we know we are about to enter into a negotiation with an international corporation, the first barrier to entry is the way this corporation does business and how it differs from our firm. Another barrier is that the person from the corporation that we are going to negotiate with may be complicated, and we must be prepared to negotiate with a difficult person.

The policies of the international corporation constitute a natural barrier that we must consider. As if this weren't enough, there is a cultural barrier, since this corporation is foreign-owned, and we may lack experience in dealing within this culture.

These are just some examples of barriers which I am sure you've experienced. The intention behind understanding the concept of barriers of negotiation is to identify them when you first enter into a negotiation. Break down the larger problem into small problems, and solve the problems in the most efficient manner. Negotiation is a continuous solution of problems between parties.

For personal barriers, there is a lot of advice in literature on how to deal with difficult people, as well as the common tactics of hard and gentle negotiators.

For cultural barriers, the golden rule is "understanding the other culture", its values and principles, as well as how these factors affect the culture of negotiation. This task is to be done without forming stereotypes.

For process barriers, it's important to understand negotiation as a science. Ask yourself, "What are the phases of the process, and what points are important in each phase?"

For natural barriers, it is important to understand which factors provide power in the negotiation, as well as the standards, time, and information.

Let's say, for example, you are about to take your family ice skating in Canada. Assume that you have a limited budget and a large family.

Upon arriving at the skating rink, the employee greets your family with a friendly smile. You realize that you must pay $9 for each admission ticket, regardless of the age. You arrive with seven persons: 2 adults and 5 children. You have the following options:

Natural Barrier: The admission price.

Cultural Barrier: You are in a foreign country.

Process Barrier: There are two "links", the employee and the supervisor.

Personal Barrier: It doesn't exist. There is good chemistry with the skating rink employee.

The options you have are:

Dealing with the natural barrier:

>1) Not saying anything about the price to the public and paying the admission price,
>2) Asking if there is some type of group discount or seniors discount

If you chose option 2, the typical reply is "there are no group discounts" or "There is a group discount for parties of more than 20 people."

If you pursue this, and ask what the price for a party of 20 people would be, and they say $6.50, what follows is for you to say, "Well, there aren't twenty of us, but we're a big family that comes often. Is there a way that we can get the group rate?" I can assure you that the reply will be, "Let me check with my supervisor." If you directly ask the supervisor, there is a good chance that you will obtain the group discount (Process Barrier - the organization, the employee and the supervisor.)

The moral of this story is that if you do not question the process of negotiation and try to break down the barriers, you will not obtain greater benefits and will lose profits at the negotiating table. This example illustrates two barriers, the natural one and the process barrier. Perhaps if the person had been difficult, the challenge would have been greater and we would have faced a "personal" barrier.

This brief example shows us how these barriers present themselves in any type of negotiation. So let's plan, analyze and synthesize the process of negotiation in its parts and identify barriers, so we can increase our power of negotiation.

We recall the great Greek philosopher and scientist, Aristotle, who said, *"Pleasure in the job puts perfection in the work."* Let us find perfection in negotiation by pursuing "best practices".

IV.9 Establishing the Standards of a Good Negotiation

To think of an ideal negotiation is Utopian. Someone always obtains a little more than the other. We can become a good negotiator if we continue to improve our actions and strategies in the mastery of the art of negotiation so that both parties come out winning.

Some typical problems in everyday negotiations in business in Mexico (Analysis of common frustrations in the process of negotiation) are:

- Both parties in the negotiation are always seeking what is best for themselves without regard for the other party.

- We only think of ourselves, "What is in for me?" and not for what's the benefit of the other party.

- If we speak frankly and show our interests, it is quite likely that the other one will take advantage of that and use the situation to gain more power in the negotiation. As a result, we will end up conceding more than we had initially expected.

- When one of the parties is a direct communicator and is too aggressive while in the process of negotiation, there will be misunderstandings or continuous frustration.

- When one of the parties is so indirect that he doesn't have the courage to face the reality of the negotiation and directly say, "We will NOT reach an agreement this way and must either pursue another type of agreement or proceed with other business and forget the matter at hand." This situation leads to continuous frustrations on the negotiation table, especially for the direct type of negotiators.

- When one party hides the real reason behind their position and delays reaching an agreement. Hiding reasons generally makes the deal go sour in the long run or produces win-lose negotiation outcomes.

These are the situations that we have observed consistently repeating themselves time and time again in negotiations in our business environment.

What do we do to avoid all this frustration and deterioration among the parties?

From the start up of the negotiation:

- Be clear and direct,
- Be honest,
- Have guts when facing the problem,
- Do not be afraid to question or ask for something,
- Be yourself,
- Don't pretend everything is fine, when the boat is sinking,
- Do not be afraid of rejection.

What can we do to standardize the characteristics of a good negotiation?

First, remember that not all negotiations are the same. They change according to the situation, number of players, the issue in question, the process, the timing, the culture, the environment, etc.

Understand the context in which the negotiation is unfolding. Initially analyze the case by itself and then compare it to previous cases, just as a reference.

Ask ourselves the following "Eight Key questions" (8 KQ's).

KQ1: Are we familiar with the client and all the decision makers?
KQ 2: Do we understand the needs of all the decision makers?
KQ 3: Can we really compete in this negotiation or are we being used as a frame of reference?
KQ 4: Can we win, and if so, will it be worth it?

KQ 5: What is the motive or reason that this negotiation is being carried out? If there are more than two, which ones are the top priorities?
KQ 6: How important or urgent is the project for the other party?
KQ 7: How relevant are we as service providers?
KQ 8: How fast is the client replying to our phone calls, mail or any type of communication?

These Eight Key Questions will serve as our guide and will help us evaluate how near or far we are from reaching an agreement with the client. For example, if we don't have an idea of how important or urgent it is to reach an agreement with the client and how relevant we are as suppliers, we may be wasting our time. Or rather, if the client takes a long time in replying to our e-mails or communications and constantly avoids us or puts things off, he is probably trying to avoid confronting us directly and saying "NO". The best thing in these cases is to be direct with the client and face reality. Pursue other business opportunities, and put whatever we are negotiating with this client on "stand by".

This is why standardizing the characteristics of a good negotiation goes beyond the tactics and strategies of negotiation. It enters the process of client prospecting and methodically assessing the business opportunity through the steps that identify the decision makers, explore the needs, and create successful presentations and proposals that lead to an effective closing.

Establishing the Process

The result of a successful negotiation can be predicted if we do our homework in the process of negotiation before starting to negotiate.

The steps that enable us to predict with high precision the expected result of a successful negotiation are:

1) Research detailed information on the other party,
2) Analyze in depth what the other party wants,
3) Research what your competitors are offering and how we can improve on that offer,
4) Find out what the timing of the deal is. How urgent is it for our client?,
5) Ensure we address all the critical points of the client's decision makers and our own,
6) Have references ready of past successful projects with other clients or similar situations,
7) Have a well-defined payment plan.

IV.10 The Key is Preparing the Negotiation

The steps to achieving an effective negotiation begin with preparation. This involves thinking ahead of time what factors will affect the negotiation we are carrying out or will carry out. Once we have defined the factors that have positive or negative impact, for example, if we identify a factor that places our negotiations at risk, we must write out actions that will diminish this risk. If we identify a factor that will be essential in enhancing our position, then we must write out what we need to do to guarantee our success. Additionally, we should think of alternatives in case we don't reach an agreement of the parties, so we understand how far to pursue this.

Many times we find ourselves at a fork in the road with two alternatives of negotiation. If we accept one, we lose the other and vice versa.

In a particular case, one situation might clearly result in short-term benefits, while the other may have mid and long-term ones. We have to choose one of the two. How do we evaluate the alternatives and action plan? A good negotiator must ask himself," How do we gain the best of both worlds? How do we use our alternatives to gain power in the negotiation? What steps do we follow to achieve a robust negotiation in this situation?"

Making a decision tree is very useful, since it allows us to "draw" different situations. We can show situation 1, with the probability of reaching an agreement or not. After that, we should ask ourselves, "What happens if we reach an agreement? What benefits do the parties gain?" Similarly the same questions apply with situation 2. In this manner, the short and long term benefits and risks of both situations can be evaluated.

Then, for both situations, we can determine the worst case scenario, the best possible result, and our expected outcome. We need to find actions to take to obtain the best scenario in both situations.

If that's not possible, we shall look for the steps that can help us reach our goal, while laying out strategies to minimize the worst of cases.

This way, the preparation of the negotiation is the key to success, followed by the strategy and actions to pursue.

IV.11 Negotiating with Difficult People

Negotiating is something that comes easily to some persons and not to others. Still, it's a skill that can be learned. Some people cannot live without negotiating and find it a fun activity. For others, negotiating is stressful and a necessary evil.

Negotiating for pleasure or with a need becomes a bigger challenge if the situation in question is difficult or if the other party is someone difficult.

Here we will define a difficult situation as in the case studies of section IV.6. It becomes extremely difficult when the other party insults us, yells, offends, intimidates or abuses his power.

These situations result from differences of opinion, thinking, interests or simply because we are facing a passive aggressive or reactive aggressive person.

The first thing we must do is deal with our emotions and not react to the other person's attack. Use positive thinking and dissociate the aggression from all personal emotions.

We can't afford ourselves the luxury of reacting aggressively or counterattacking, since the other party will only react more aggressively. There is a metaphor that Professor Ury from Harvard University told me about one day. "Go out on the balcony and reflect, when you receive aggression from the other party."

This idea of going out to the balcony means to change mental channels or take a time out and mentally evade the aggression, or as we mentioned in section IV.6, "count sheep" when the other party offends us.

Being objective is a blessing in moments of aggression. It allows us not to react negatively. It is also good to be able to let time pass, thereby allowing the other party to cool down.

We must think about the objectives we are trying to achieve in the negotiation and focus our thoughts on the success we will achieve and block out the other person's attacks.

Once we have controlled our reactions of anger, rage or envy, the next step is to surprise the other party instead of attacking.

Ask yourself what the interest behind the position is. In other words, understand what the other party needs. It's important here to think like the other party, forgetting our interests and looking deep down to see what the other party needs.

Once we understand what the other party needs, the art lies in finding a solution that benefits them and ties in to our interests so we can reach a win-win negotiation.

In summary, we must first control our own reactions, followed by understanding what the client needs, proposing solutions and finally, tying those into our own interests so we can secure a productive and successful negotiation.

IV.12 Negotiation of a Perishable Product Past its Expiration Date

The firm XYZ sold a lot of products that had a specific shelf life. The sales of the product were such that the salespeople had never concerned themselves with disposing of products whose shelf life had expired.

Despite this, the director of firm XYZ, Peter, asks the sales director, John, to place 6 truckloads of expired product during the Christmas season.

This was a challenge for John, since the distribution channel for expired products is different from the distribution channel of perishable products.

John was aware that some businesses sell expired and damaged product. But this market niche was new and unfamiliar to him. (This is a legal practice in some countries.)

John decided to go knocking on doors, since his challenge was to place 6 truckloads of the expired product three days before Christmas.

The alternatives for firm XYZ before John went out to sell the expired product were:

> 1) Pay for the waste management services to remove the product and the transportation to the waste disposal site,
> 2) Donate the product to the community through churches or community centers,
> 3) Sell it to a shop or firm that distributed damaged or expired product.

The product had a cost of $10 per unit. If the firm opted for option 1, it lost the $10 of revenue plus $2 per unit for transportation and waste removal, adding up to $12 per unit.

If the firm opted for option 2, it would only lose $10 per unit plus the cost of transportation to community centers or the church, which was minimal.

The most attractive option for firm XYZ was option 3, sell them at any price, preferably at $5 per unit.

With this prior information, John sets out to find the highest bidder.

There are firms on the market that deal with selling damaged products we'll call "waste". While looking for these firms, John finds firm ABC. At firm ABC most of the product line was waste, while the product that XYZ had to offer was in perfect condition. It had just recently expired.

John offered his products to the purchaser at ABC, Rudy, and he replied, "I think your product is great. We'll just have to talk to the owner of the business." Right then and there, Rudy called Joe and said, "Joe, the salesman from firm XYZ, which is known for the quality of their products, is here, and he has 6 truckloads of product he's offering us at a good price. The only thing is that it's expired." Joe replies, "Fine, let me talk to the salesman, please." John starts with, "Hello, Joe. What do you think about this opportunity? At XYZ, we usually don't have expired products, and if we reach an agreement, we'd have another channel for expired products. Are you interested?" Joe replies, "Yes, a lot. I am out of town on business with other firms in this market, and we might be able to sell them the rest of the product. What do you say you give me all the merchandise at $2 a unit and I'll pay you in three days when I get back?" John replies, "Dear Joe, you know the regular price is $10 a unit, and at $2, it's better to give it away in the community. How about $5?" "Well, let's meet each other halfway and settle the price at $3.50 a unit", Joe said. "For the sake of wrapping this up, you can have it at $4, on the condition that you pay us right away", John counters. Joe says, "I accept your price of $4 dollars, but you'll have to wait three days for payment." John takes the risk with this new vendor and says, "It's a **Deal**. We don't take any returns."

The date of payment comes around, and Joe is apparently not in his office. Rudy tells John, "I'm sorry to tell you that Joe won't pay you until next year, and what's more, he's going to return the product that expired more than 8 months ago." This represented just 1/8 of the lot of the 6 truckloads of product.

John asks, "Can I speak to Joe?" John asks Joe, "What happened to our deal?" Joe replies, "We are talking about a small portion of product, and don't even bother picking it up. We'll dispose of it."

To this statement John replies, "Very well, Joe. I am sending for a check right now based on what we agreed upon, and whatever you want to return that's expired, we'll take care of and distribute in the community. Our trucks will pick it up this morning." John hangs up. Less than 3 minutes later, Joe calls John back, and as if nothing had happened says, "Hi John, what's new? I think I went too far. The product is not so bad. Send for the check. It's no big deal, and there will be no returns."

What happened with this negotiation? The **Process** was such that in the beginning of the negotiation, John had less power of negotiation, and Joe, as a good negotiator, got a good price. Nonetheless, John did not let himself be intimidated or pressured and got a good price for the product. Joe probably tried to manipulate the situation once he had the product in his warehouses and tried to change the rules of the game with John (**Process**) to try to obtain an additional discount.

By not wanting to return the expired **Product,** he had probably sold it elsewhere and tried to manipulate the situation by making John believe that he was doing him a favor by disposing of the most heavily expired product and aiding John who wouldn't have to send a truck to pick it up.

John's strategy of not backing down from his strong position and utilizing the tactic of ultimatum was the key. John was upset because at the closing Joe had firmly agreed to payment in three days, and no changes were to be made in scope. For John, the negotiation had become a negotiation of principles. It was more important for John to sustain his position since his power of negotiation was greater than when he had started knocking on doors.

This prompted Joe to call him back three minutes after their conversation ended. This was perhaps because Joe realized that John was a reliable supplier, and that the product, though expired, was in good condition and better than the average of his products.

Returning a portion of product that had the earliest expiration might set a precedent and cause them to lose future business opportunities with firm XYZ.

If we analyze the alternatives to a non-agreement for Joe, at that moment they were:

> 1) Not accepting a portion of the lot would cost him future business with a reliable supplier like firm XYZ,
> 2) Returning all the product was not profitable, since he would have to incur transportation costs and the cost of opportunity,
> 3) Accepting John's offer was his best alternative.

Among other lessons to be learned here, it is good to understand the **Power** of negotiation of the parties and to what extent the other party starts to manipulate us. The negotiation of principles is vital in this case. The ethics and honesty of the parties is the driving force of long-term relationships. In this case both parties, John as well as Joe, were interested in a long term one. John could use them as an alternative channel of distribution for expired Products, and Joe would be the best reliable source of **Products** with better quality than what he was currently selling and at a competitive price. Here we saw how the **Person** (John, Joe, Rudy), the **Process** (analysis of alternatives for the parties), the **Product**, the **Problem** (expired product), the **Power** (of the parties) have an effect on the **Power** of negotiation.

I invite you to apply the concepts we've mentioned here on your projects and everyday negotiations and I assure you that you will exceed your **Prognosis** each time.

This case may not apply in all countries. Since selling perishable products past its expiration date is not legal in all countries. This case is only used as another example to illustrate the 6 P's of the negotiation methodology.

"Pride is the complement of ignorance." - Fontenelle

Chapter V

A general perception of the buying process in the United States is that when a buyer is requesting lots of product or service information, he is most likely to make a buying decision within a short period of time (sense of urgency). A common behavior is pictured in the following anecdote when an American seller is dealing with a Mexican buyer that frequently requested a lot of information from the American seller within a short period of time.

On one occasion, we had a situation with a Mexican firm where the owner called our Houston office several times requesting information about our workshops. He called almost twice a week over a period of one month. After he received the information, we never heard from him again.

What happened? Most likely the Mexican buyer wanted: 1) to obtain information for next year's budget approval, 2) to make a buyer's comparison chart for the record, or 3) to obtain an estimate from a third party for benchmarking similar in-house services. Whatever the Mexican buyer wanted, one thing is certain: a sense of urgency from the Mexican buyer does not carry the same meaning as a sense of urgency for the American seller. Furthermore, the expression "urgent" is commonly used in Mexico and is not reserved for emphatic use as in the States. The inexperienced American seller can easily be misled by behaviors from the Mexican buyer, resulting in immense frustration.

Efficient Techniques for Successful Negotiating

"When we carry out a purchase with our emotions upfront and under pressure, we place the value on the negotiation table at risk."
Dr. Habib Chamoun-Nicolás

This chapter contains the following topics:

V.1 The 14 Factors that Influence Successful Negotiations

V.2 The 14 Efficient Techniques for Negotiating Large Projects

V.3 How Do You Gain Power in High-Profitability Projects?

V.4 Power and International Negotiations

V.1 The 14 Factors that Influence Successful Negotiations

Two key factors that diminish the power of negotiation are: a) not defining the scope of work and b) lack of experience.

The solutions to these negative factors are communication and preparation, respectively. In the following chart V.1, we list the 14 factors that diminish the power of negotiation and some possible solutions.

14 Factors that Diminish the Power of Negotiation	Solutions
1. Lack of definition in the scope of work. 2. Assuming the expectations of the other party without writing them in "black and white" in a document.	**COMMUNICATION** • Clearly write up what is included and what is not in the products and services you sell.
3. Minimal or lack of experience of one of the negotiating parties. 4. Failing to put the agreement in writing. 5. Lack of follow up to client visits.	**PREPARATION** • Educate by example. • Use references and standards of the industrial sector that the client belongs to. **COMMUNICATION** • Adopt and implement a control system for documentation. • Draw up a document or letter of intent together with the client about the work to be conducted. • Write a win/win contract. • Have weekly meetings and minutes on the progress of the work and assess progress. Avoid renegotiating.

Chart V.1 The 14 Factors that Diminish the Power of Negotiation

[1] Research on the culture and factors of influence conducted by Dr. Jeswald Salacuse of the Harvard Negotiation Program and Tufts University. Research in Mexico conducted by Dr. Habib Chamoun, with the express permission of Dr. Jeswald W. Salacuse.

14 Factors that Diminish the Power of Negotiation	Solutions
6. Lack of understanding of non-verbal signals from other party. 7. Not taking into consideration cultural differences.	**COMMUNICATION** • Study and understand the cultures of the other parties.[1] • Do not generalize and try to understand how to proceed in specific cases. General notes on some cultures: • Latin culture: Culture of relationships. • Anglo Saxon culture: Culture of contracts. • Japanese culture: Decision making by consensus. • Chinese culture: Steadfast in negotiations.
8. Scarce information 9. Surprise (when the client catches you off guard). 10. Individualism: "I, my, mine, with me..."	**PREPARATION** Prepare yourself with information on the: • Market • Client • Opportunity • Competition • product/service • generate/create options **TEAM WORK** • Promote team work in your company and your client's.
11. No taking into account the gender differences. 12. Close to closing, but we don't close. The "almost closing."	**UNDERSTANDING THE CLIENT'S NEEDS** Understand the factors that may be different by gender: • Feminine - From specific to general. • Masculine – From general to specific **DEFINE** • Close the circle. • It's over, right or wrong. • Evaluate the cost/benefit.
13. Widespread and quick concessions untied to any objective.	**CLOSING STRATEGIES** • Do not concede unless you have an objective to fulfill. • Do not speculate. • When you concede, do so slowly and in small amounts, but make sure this is tied into a goal of the negotiation. • Even if something has no value to you, emphasize the value it has when conceding it to the other party. Otherwise he will not appreciate the concession.
14. Having a blank slate mind as you approach the negotation table.	**PREPARATION** • Arrive at the negotiating table with a defined objective and another exit objective and you will close the deal.

V.2 The 14 Efficient Techniques for Negotiating Large Projects

(The information in section V.2 is based on the article *"Learning to Close Good Deals"*. Entrepreneur Magazine. July, 2002.)

We present a summary of the 14 efficient techniques for negotiating large projects in diagram V.2.

Business Development

Preparation
Defining objectives
Putting information in order
Dominating the market
State validity
Offer options
Avoid suprises
Separate results
Seek empathy
Follow up
Learn about standards
Identify mutual solutions
Recognize the Closing moment
Identify your skills

Robust Negotiations

Developing Long Term Relationships

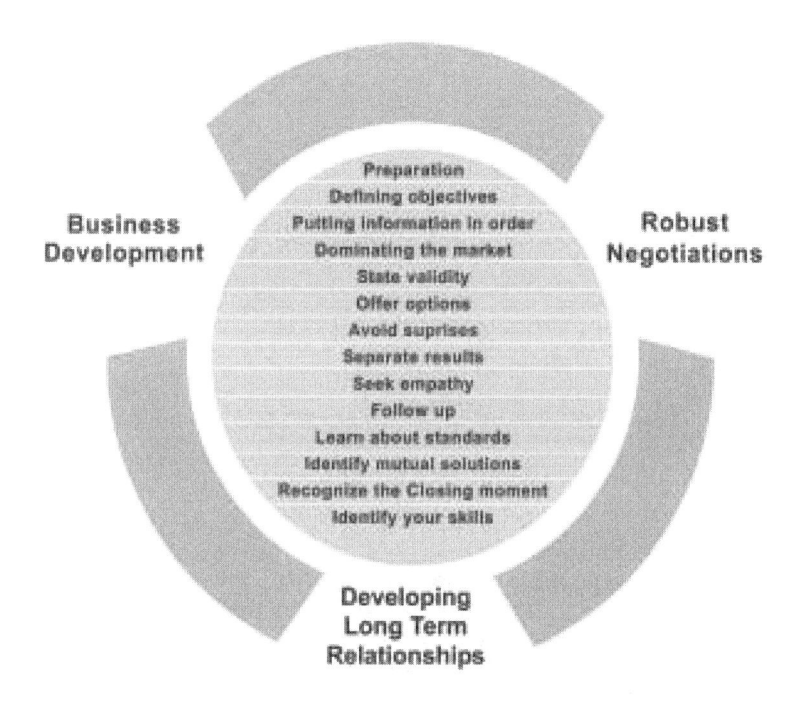

Diagram V.2 The 14 Efficient Techniques for Negotiating Large Projects

1st Preparation:

Preparation is essential in any negotiation process. William Ury, professor of Harvard University, states that for every minute of negotiation, a minimum of one minute of preparation is required.

It is vitally important that we know "who" makes the decisions within the organization with which we are to negotiate, as well "what" needs each decision maker has.

Knowledge of key factors that might influence the negotiation, such as the range of discounts that one may offer, if the price is negotiable, is essential.

Let's prepare ourselves on the following aspects:

- **Person, Process, Product, Power,**
- Number of Issues,
- Number of **Persons,**
- Culture,
- Explore the Aspirations and Expectations of Others.
- Separate the **Person** from the **Problem** (Fisher, Ury and Patton, 1991),
- Understand the Cultural Impact,
- Understand the Environment and Context of the Negotiation.

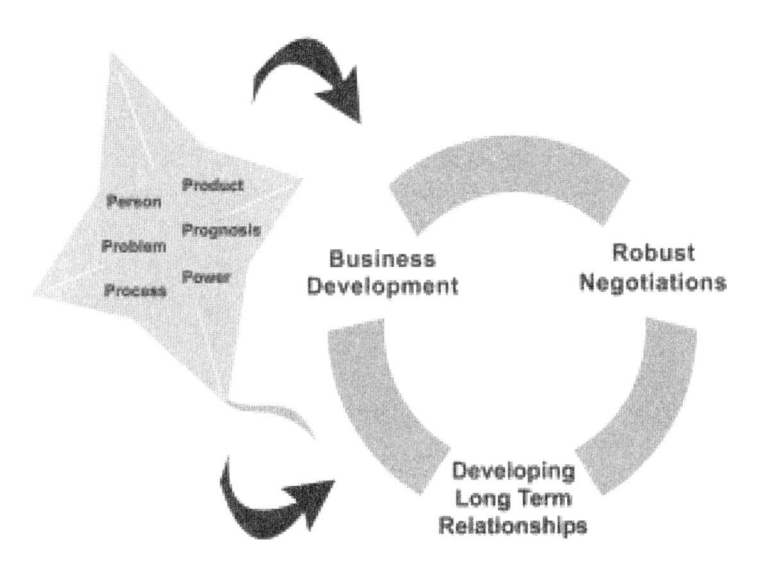

Diagram V.3 Preparing for the Negotiation while Covering Every Angle Ensures Long Lasting Relationships

2nd Definition of Objectives:

Determine if you are seeking to close a general deal and subsequently negotiate the specifics, or if it is convenient to start with the details. If the purpose, for example, is to establish a strategic alliance, then the most effective method would be to negotiate on general terms. On the other hand, if your objective is to negotiate a specific purchase, then you will have to negotiate the specifics first.

Among other things, we need to:

- Know the in and outs of the objective before visiting the client,
- Define our objectives and learn about the other party's objectives,

- Remember that objectives can change,
- Not assume the objectives of the counterpart.

3rd Organize the Information:

List the main interests and arrange them in order of importance. I am referring to interests, such as the reason behind the position of both parties (Fisher, Ury and Patton, 1991), and their needs. This way, you will be able to present a more convincing position to the counterpart. For example, perhaps the price is not as important as the delivery date and quality. Thus, the order of importance would be delivery, quality and price.

Additional tips:

- Research the aspirations and expectations of the parties,
- Become familiar with the range of discounts (Fisher, Ury and Patton, 1991),
- Find the alternatives to a non-agreement between the parties (Fisher, Ury and Patton, 1991),
- Find solutions that will satisfy the interest of the parties,
- Analyze the impact of the alternatives of sales or leasing of a product from A to B and what impact they will have on C (see Diagram V.4).

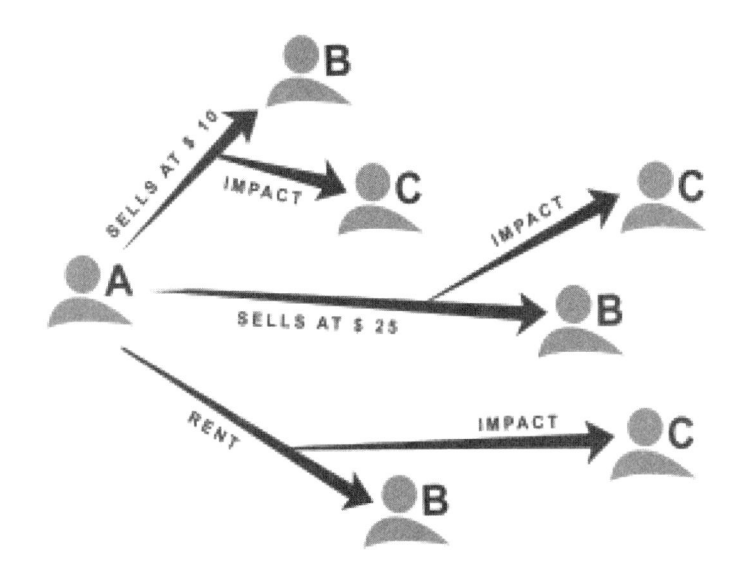

Diagram V.4 Analysis of the impact of A selling or leasing a product to B and the impact on C.

4th Dominating your Market:

It's important to understand the territory in which you are negotiating. If your counterpart is a client who belongs to the automobile industry, which is very cost competitive, you will have to immediately assume that one of his priorities will be the price. If, on the other hand, the client belongs to the pharmaceutical industry, his priority will probably be product safety.

As tips to achieve dominance in your market, we recommend you:

- Understand the business relationships between the players in the specific environment (see Diagram V.5),
- Understand the business models,
- Find synergies.

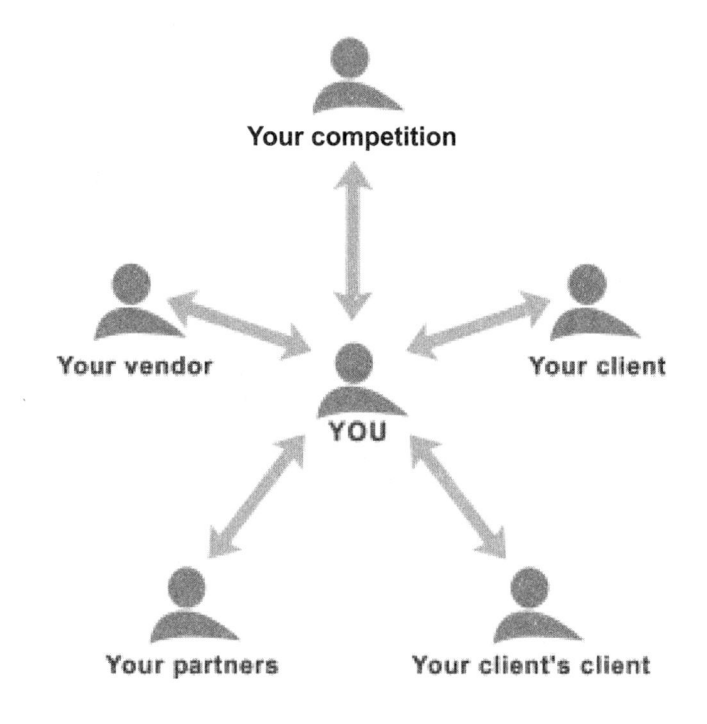

Diagram V.5 Business Relationships between the Players in the Environment (Brandenburger and Nalebuff, 1998)

5th State the Validity:

In any proposal, establishing the limit of time during which the offer is valid is a way of proving if the other party is interested in an efficient closing. When the stated date comes up, the quote expires and the rules of negotiation will change.

Remember to establish:
- A time limit,
- An ultimatum (take it or leave it strategy),
- How? When? With whom?

6th Offer Options:

Propose alternatives that your client can analyze without commitment. What happens if I pay in two months? What is the price if this is a cash operation? What happens if I don't want the rugs that come with the car?

Options are characterized as:

- Being specific to the business opportunity in question,
- Offering flexibility,
- Depending on the case, situation, type, context,
- Depending on the culture.

7th Avoid Surprises:

The worst thing that can happen at the negotiation table is when the client surprises you with a position you had not foreseen. How do you avoid that? You can do so with adequate preparation, by visualizing each possible scenario and by being creative.

Avoid:

- Letting "chaos" fall over the process,
- Getting "picked off base" (baseball),
- Having "the rug pulled out from under you".

Remember that there are cultures that negotiate under chaos, while others prefer order.

8th Separate the Results:

Establish agreements without linking them to other negotiations. If you have made a concession to reach an agreement, avoid having the other party tie this concession to another agreement. An example of this occurs when the other party makes the proposal, "We are giving you a lot of work, so you should concede on something. That way we can give you more work." Do not set a precedent!

Some tips:

- Research the links that form the negotiation (Watkins, 2002),
- Avoid constant haggling over the price,
- Do not set a precedent (Each project is different and unique.),
- Each negotiation should be "autonomous.",
- Do not tie the results of one project to another, unless you are going to do so to increase your power of negotiation,
- Let bygones be bygones,
- Remember, this is not wholesaling.

9th Find Empathy:

Build empathy with your counterpart. What follows has been proven by researchers in negotiation from Harvard University:

In a cooperative negotiation, where both parties are friends and have as a common goal of reaching a win-win agreement, the result is that the "pie" (the benefits) increases for both of them (Fisher, Ury and Patton, 1991).

On the contrary, in a competitive negotiation where the parties are adversaries, the pie has so many divisions that value is left on the negotiation table, and the parties do not benefit as much as they could.

In conclusion, in a cooperative negotiation, both parties not only get a bigger piece of the pie, but they also increase its size.

Some tips:

- Pursue a long term relationship,
- Understand the influence of the culture,
- Don't expect everyone to be like you,
- Separate the person from the problem.

10th Follow Up:

Design an action plan for the negotiation. This is a plan with steps and tactical activities to carry out, based on the strategies and alternatives involved. Also include tactics such as strategies for an exit, for not putting pressure on yourself or long term thinking.

Find solutions that:

- Differentiate you from the competition,
- Provide added value,
- Do not forget post-sale service.

11th Know the Standards:

It's important to have reference values and to know how and when to use them. Reference values are determined by the market. For example, if you conduct your business in the auto industry, do you know how much a 2004 model of a specific type costs? This is just a parameter or benchmark.

Ask yourself the following before you offer your client your consulting services:

- Who says I'm too expensive? Expensive in comparison to whom?
- Who says I am pricing myself way below the market?
- Will I quote the unit price = $/ man hours?
- Will I quote the lump sum price = sum of unit costs?

12th Identify Solutions:

When the following situations arise:

- Multiple options are possible,
- Points of mutual agreement are identified,
- Several negotiation items could be packaged together.

Ask yourself the following questions:

What would happen if I don't reach an agreement with the other party? What is the worst that could happen? What consequences will my counterpart face if we don't reach an agreement?

13th Recognize the Moment of Closing:

When a client asks a lot of technical, very specific questions, it is generally a signal that he is ready to close. The key then is to have him close with you and not a competitor.

Ideas

- The salesperson must have a closing mentality,
- The closing is a window of opportunity in time that opens and closes quickly,
- A sale has not been made until every last detail has been closed.

14th Identify Your Talents:

If you have a weakness and recognize that you concede too much when you are under pressure, you can create an alternative for the closing. Use a third person whose negotiation characteristics are tougher than yours.

Instead, you can program yourself to use the following phrases:

- Do not make concessions,
- Do not give anything unless asked and always in exchange for something,
- Do not concede too quickly,
- Do not give extra information,
- Do not make a commitment until you are sure you can deliver,
- Let the other person talk,
- Generate options.

Ideas

- Ask yourself if it is possible (cultural). Don't say yes to everything!,
- If you can't bear the load, form alliances!,
- Remember that delivering is more important than selling,
- Focus on customer service,
- Propose to secure repeat clients.

V.3 How Do You Gain Power in High-Profitability Projects?

Beyond the 10 P's of the CHAMOUN sales methodology*, that introduces the concepts from various methodologies (Bosworth, 1995; Hanan, 1995; Miller and Heiman, 1986;

Rackham, 1988; Siebel, 1996; Wilson, 1995; Ziglar, 1996.), we have observed that for more complex and sophisticated projects, we can efficiently use the principles and concepts of the Adventace sales methodology. This one stands out for its focus on complex and high profitability accounts.

The Adventace sales methodology exceeds others in the literature by increasing the salesperson's power of negotiation for several reasons: 1) It offers an action plan that helps the buyer make a decision that makes it easy to achieve the desired results, 2) It focuses its efforts on the decision maker with the most power to those who have access to power and looks for a strategy that will provide an entry point and expansion for the account and the relationship.

In this chapter, with the express permission of Adventace, we briefly present the steps of this methodology.

First of all, this methodology helps us create a vision of an environment of high performance sales.

It begins by understanding: 1) The model of how clients carry out their purchases, followed by 2) the methodology of sales and operations, and 3) finally integrating the corporate culture and the continuous improvement at all levels of the organization, including the executive top management.

This method is based on a frame of reference of knowledge and skills that the salesperson must acquire, including the knowledge of the business environment of the buyer and the capabilities of the salesperson.

This model comprises five phases or steps of how clients make their purchases, as well as eight steps of the visit to the client. The five phases of the purchasing cycle are (see Diagram A):

1) Subconscious Critical Business Issue of the Buyer (CBI)
2) Discovery of the Critical Business Issues of the Buyer (CBI)
3) Analysis and Proof
4) Risk and Value
5) Implementation

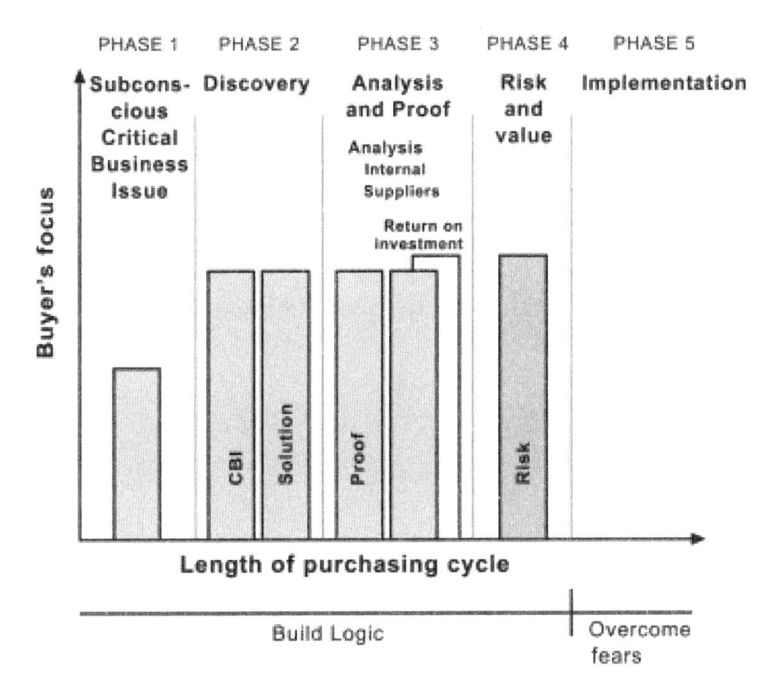

Diagram A. The Five Phases of the Purchasing Cycle, According to the Adventace Methodology

During phases 1 to 3, the methodology focuses on increasing, in a logical fashion, the evidence of solutions to the critical business issues of the buyer. This is focused on preserving the motivation in the buyer's behavior towards a decision that favors our solution by the time he reaches phase 4 (Risk).

155

You must remember that the client typically negotiates the price in phase 4, and as we logically build our case in phases 1 thru 3, we can build support to increase our power of negotiation and avoid haggling.

Another tool that this methodology uses is an "action plan" that helps the client make a decision (This plan is applied in the latter part of phase 2). This is merely a scientific methodology based on the discovery of the critical business issues (CBI) of the decision makers in the buyer's firm. To find the buyer's critical business issues and its causes, it uses questions regarding the evolution of solutions or the restatement of new solutions. This series of questions helps the decision makers arrive at the final point of purchase, consciously and logically, based on the expected result.

The eight steps of the visit to the client are (see Diagram B):

    1) Prospecting and alignment,
    2) Establishing the goals of the visit,
    3) Foresight of a competent message,
    4) Development of needs,
        a. Evolution,
        b. Restatement,
5) Determination of causes and effects of the buyer's critical business issues (CBI),
6) Determination of the buyer's level of power,
        a. Promoter,
        b. Promoter with access to power,
        c. Final decision maker,
7) Negotiation for access to power:
        a. Proof to gain access to power ,
        b. Qualifying the purchasing process and defining the plan for action,

8) Issuing letters of understanding,
    a. To the promoter,
    b. To the promoter with access to power,
    c. Discussion of the proposal,
    d. Winning approval.

*The 10 P's of the CHAMOUN Methodology (from the book, "Business Development", 3rd edition)

- Prepare yourself,
- Picture the different customer decision makers and influence entities,
- Position yourself in one of the Chamoun's four types of salesman model, according to your customer (or service provider) relationship, see diagram II.4,
- Proof of a profitable return on investment, linking the value added by products and services to the customer needs and wants,
- Put down on paper extensive list of strengths and weaknesses,
- Propose successful strategies,
- Plan actions to make it happen,
- Preview of a tryout exercise with a pioneering test
- Present and Propose to customers successfully (Shipley Associates Proposal Guide, 2001),
- Predict and Proclaim success.

```
                                                    Sales cycle
┌─────────────────────────────────────────────────┐ ┌─────────────────────┐
│ Plan for the account,                            │ ■ Execute the plan of action
│ Identifying the opportunity.  Market research    │   (For qualification and control
│                                                  │   of the sales cylce.)
│ 1  Prospection and alignment                     │
│                                                  │ Phase II
│            Visit to the client                   │ ■ Visit the decision makers
│ 2  Establishing the goals of the visit           │   with influence.
│                                                  │ ■ Determine their CBI's
│ 3  Providing the competent message               │   and capabilities
│                                                  │
│    Developing needs.                             │ Phase III
│ 4  Solution Evolution                            │ ■ Proof
│    Solution Re-evolution                         │ ■ Establish parameters to
│                                                  │   measure success.
│ 5  Determining cause and effect                  │ ■ Research and analysis
│                                                  │   (billed to buyer)
│ 6  Determine the levels of power of the purchaser│ ■ Justification of value
│                                                  │ ■ Legal reviews
│      Promoter          Power Promoter            │ ■ Technical analysis
│ 7    Negotiating proof Qualify the purchasing    │ ■ Discussion of proposals
│      for access        process
│      to power          Define Action Plan        │ Phase IV
│                                                  │ ■ Obtaining a YES
│      Send letter of    Send letter of            │ ■ Intiating the implementation.
│ 8    understanding     understanding to
│      to the promoter   the Power Promoter
└─────────────────────────────────────────────────┘
```

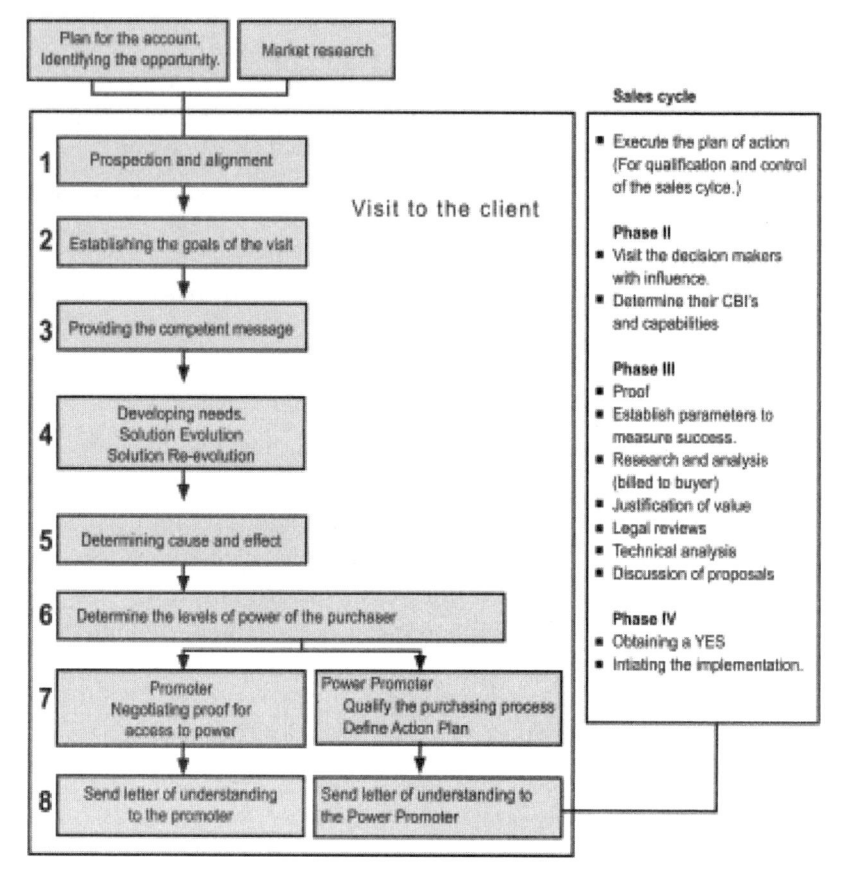

Diagram B. The Eight Steps of the Visit to the Client According to Adventace.

If we follow the Adventace methodology with the following four steps (I, II, III, and IV) we can increase our negotiating power.

Step I:

Integrate the buyer's business environment with the salesperson capabilities in order to satisfy buyer's critical business issues (CBI's).

Find main causes to Buyers' CBI's.

Align specific capabilities to product and services characteristics (see Diagram C)

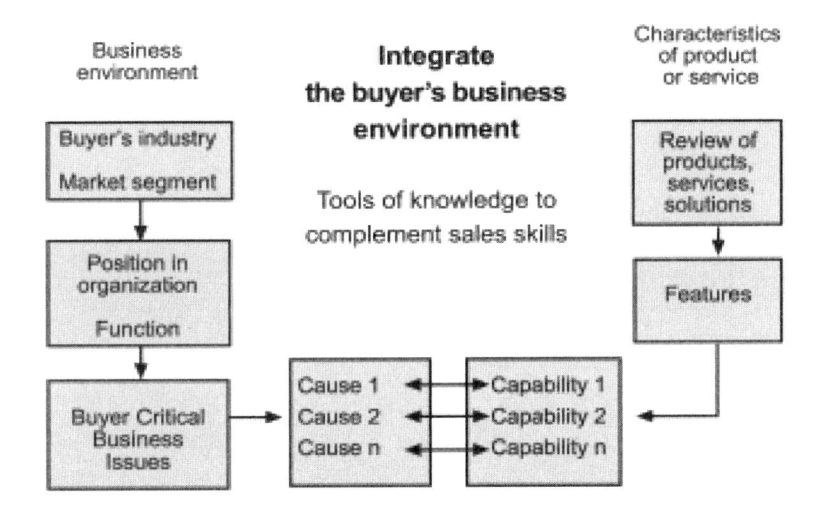

Diagram C. Integration of the Buyer's Business Environment with the Capabilities of the Salesperson as a Tool of Knowledge.

Step II:

Classifies buyers into three types: the promoter, the promoter with access to power and the final decision maker.

Analyzes the critical business issues (CBI) of each buyer.

Links each buyer to his critical business issues (CBI) and their causes, to find the cause and effect interrelation at the different levels of decision makers.

Defines a line of power within the organization for the decision makers.

Concentrates the efforts on the strategic access to power and ascending to it, with the objective of reaching the decision makers that are above the line of power, as displayed in diagram D.

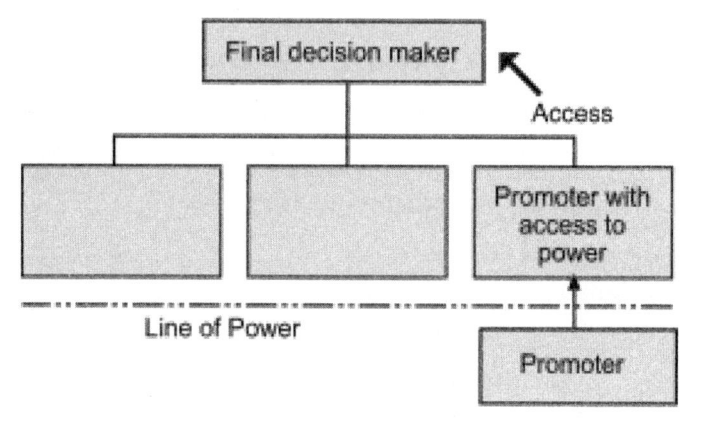

Diagram D. Decision Makers according to Adventace.

Characteristics of the decision maker:

- Promoter
    - Under the line of power
    - Provides information
- Mentor
    - Intelligence for the organization
- Promoter with access to power
    - Above the line of power
    - Agrees to introduce you to the buyers above the line of power
- Final decision maker
    - Takes the purchasing decision
    - May not influence it; just takes the decision
    - Signs the contract

Step III:

In the phase of discovery, it is important to find the critical business issues (CBI) (i.e., loss of market share, value of company stock, decrease in sales, etc.) and analyze how they are interconnected.

Step IV:

In the phase proof and qualifications, it is important to ask the client if causes a,b,c linked to qualifications x, y, z could satisfy the critical business issues (CBI) cbi1, cbi2 and cbi3. Proof could be a case history of success with other clients, references, or trends or benchmarking within the client's industry.

It is vital to confirm with the buyer if the qualifications would eliminate the critical business issues.

The Adventace methodology aligns itself with the 5 phases of the purchasing process as explained in these steps:

1) It is easier to win the project in question if we start our relationship with the buyer from the onset, in phase 1 while prospecting. In this phase, the critical business issue (CBI), lies in the subconscious mind of the buyer and he may not bring it up since he doesn't know how to solve it. We can help him determine the causes of the CBI and find a solution.

2) When we find the buyer's critical business issue (CBI) and show the causes and the solution alongside the capabilities of our products and services, we start to gain power in the negotiation, and above all, mold this into a "course of action", helping the buyer make a decision.

3) The objections to the closing of the sale can be avoided before they become objections in phases 3 and 4, by offering value and demonstrating the return on the investment.

4) Logic will defeat the fear of making the purchasing decision. This is the logic that is built in phases 1 to 3, and will help us have elements of negotiation with the buyer.

5) The implementation is advanced when the proposal is discussed with the client before the delivery date, providing an opportunity to include any observation from the buyer.

In summary, the complexity of these sales justifies finding new tools and solutions with this methodology of "8 Steps to the Visit to the Client", and a system for exploring the critical business issues (CBI) and their causes. It allows us to link these to the capabilities of the characteristics of the products and services of the salesperson, so these and the success stories can be analytically verified, resulting in a course of action that will aid the buyer in making the purchasing decision.

In this manner, after having followed the 10 P's of the CHAMOUN sales methodology. We can include the concepts of the Adventace sales methodology in complex sales and increase our power of negotiation.

V.4 Power and International Negotiations

Massive asymmetries of power turn negotiations into very difficult ones for the weaker party. It is easy to say "no negotiation is possible", but these inequalities generate a difficult, though not impossible situation.

As one acquires more experience in negotiations, one learns that **Power** is not something that is had and stored, but rather it is something that is used and can be increased or diminished according to how intelligent we are in applying it. The use of adequate strategies strengthens **Power** within the negotiation process. Also, the adequate flow of information can allow us to increase our power within the process.

From an optimistic point of view, we visualize two parties within the negotiation process: a weak one and a strong one. With skill and expertise, the weak one may reduce the differences in **Power** and achieve an asymmetry in the relationship. For this reason, it is not always the strong party who takes advantage of the weaker one. It is just that the weaker party has to use the best possible strategies to even out this disparity.

In combination with this, as we've mentioned previously, **Power** is constantly changing. **Power** is the ability to influence or move the decision of the other party in the desired direction. Furthermore, a person has **Power** in a negotiation if he exercises influence, is persuasive or shows leadership. In summation, in the context of this book, **Power** is analyzed as the "ability to influence".

Other experiences have proven to us that the weaker party is generally more powerful than he may appear, and the stronger party is weaker than was assumed in the beginning.

We see these situations when we approach the analysis of specific cases and interests where power will lie with the party that offers it and how it is given to his opponent.

One of the most common errors is panic for **Power.** It does not allow us to plan or establish the objective that we want in the negotiation. A second error is not defining properly "what is being pursued", because without this, we cannot establish an adequate strategy.

When we speak of strategies, we should make a distinction between the strategies that we use to obtain power and the sources that generate power. The types of sources, according to Lewicki, Saunders and Minton are: information and experience control over resources and the position within the structure of the organization. When we analyze strategies, it is in part according to the psychologist D. McClelland, who created the diagram called the "classification of the orientation to power" that contains four strategies which the weaker party can use to face this challenge. Building upon this classification, Professor Dr. Salacuse took these four paths and called them "the four major strategies to acquire power and achieve objectives in international systems", labeling them: dependence, autonomy, vindication and communication. (Diagram V.6)

The Strategies to Acquire Power	Sources That Generate Power
Dependence	Information and experience,
Autonomy	Control over resources,
Vindication	Position within the structure of
Community	the organization.

Diagram V.6 The Four Major Strategies, according to Dr. Salacuse

Dependence

There is a direct relation between the weak party and the third party that will be used in the negotiation. The weak party will seek out support among other countries, building an agreement of dependence and relations. This is a form of finding protection and power in a third party that has it and that is recognized by our opponent.

In the international context, this occurs when small countries seek the help, for example, of their colonists to obtain financial, military or technological support.

Autonomy

Another strategy is maintaining autonomy because of the costs that might arise from the strategy of dependence. This strategy does not mean the abolishment of interaction with other parties, but that, in order to preserve autonomy, it is involved in many negotiations. This autonomy allows for the possibility of offering a position without ties that might prove more attractive to the opponent, awakening the interest of that party and the need for an alliance.

Vindication

This is obviously a strategy easily used by the party with the most power, which consists of showing the consequences of not fulfilling the initiative. However, the weaker party might find a way to interpret this and display the possible problems and consequences that will result if there is no complement with a minimum consideration of its needs. This is a dangerous strategy, since it involves a certain degree of threat that is not directly expressed.

Community

Finally, we can be a part of a community that supports our existence and beliefs as part of the group. We see ourselves supported by the resources and relationships of the community. The strong party is supporting this organization that allows us to use the strengths of that party within the organization, making it impossible for the strong party to exercise power over the weaker party.

In summary, there is a clear necessity to shed the feeling of panic when we face an international negotiator with more power. Additionally, it is important to know beforehand what we want and determine the possibility of using any of these four strategies that pave the way for us, as well as what form of communication we will establish during the negotiation. It also depends on the position that we establish, defining the relationship and the form in which the different points of the negotiation will be conducted. This implies a great deal of work, and as a result, a focused preparation.

Appendix

A.1 How to Achieve Robust Negotiations with Latin Americans

Negotiation with a global vision leads to better deals for both parties.

Learn how to build better bridges between the Americas.

If we examine the cultural differences in negotiation and the factors that affect the negotiation style between the USA and Latin American countries such as Mexico, we will better understand our neighbors and do a better job of building long-term business and personal relationships. The reflections and findings reported in this Appendix are based on the research conducted by the author using Dr. Jeswald Salacuse's model of 10 factors affecting the negotiation style (See Salacuse, J.W. *Making Global Deals- What Every Executive Should Know About Negotiating Abroad*: Times Business, 1992.) It is not the intention by reporting these findings to create a stereotype or to predispose ourselves when entering into negotiations. This would only serve to increase existing cultural barriers!

It is our intention to reduce the gap in our communication and increase the respect for cultural differences. Remember the saying, "When in Rome do as the Romans do."? I would suggest adding the phrase "without compromising your values", so it becomes "Do as the Romans do in Rome without compromising your values".

As discussed earlier, a vision of global negotiation could be achieved by breaking down any negotiation into six fundamental elements.

People	"the players",
Process	the negotiation process and its parts,
Power	the sources of power,
Product	the element of what is being negotiated or the business opportunity to be analyzed,
Problem	the matter in dispute or conflict,
Prognosis	the forecast element.

The 6 P's are analyzed extensively in existing publications. The main focus of this Appendix is the P of **People**. However, for the sake of thoroughness, let us mention briefly the 6 P's. The **Product**, is sometimes referred to as the business opportunity, and has been carefully analyzed by many authors of sales methodologies. Most of the methodologies help the readers concentrate on analyzing the opportunity, the decision makers, the influencers and the decision making process. They also help define the client's needs and wants. In summary, the methodologies help the sellers to find out if there is a real opportunity, if he can compete, if he can win and if it is worth the effort of pursuing the specific opportunity. These sales methodologies help the seller understand the buyer's vision of the decision making process as he is buying (Adventace workshops materials, 2004; Bosworth, 1995; Hanan, 1995; Miller and Heiman, 1986; Rackham, 1988; Seibel, 1996; Wilson, 1995; Ziglar, 1991).

The **Process**, or the negotiation **Process**, is also discussed in depth in literature. The act of negotiation is a time consuming effort. It is not a single directed activity without interrelation. Instead, it is a continuous **Process** that needs to be understood fully by all the negotiating parties. Sometimes understanding is more important to the process than the substance we are negotiating. Negotiators, having the tendency to focus on substance, can easily forget the process and fail to obtain win/win negotiations. There are many known treatises that explain the science of negotiation and its complexities (Breslin and Rubin, 1999; Nierenberg, 1995; Pruitt, 1991; Raiffa, 2000; Walton, 1965; Watkins, 2002; Young, 1994; Zartman, 1991).

The P of **Power** is the **Power** of negotiation and many authors have explained the sources of **Power** and the importance of **Power** over the negotiating parties and the outcome (Cohen, 1982; Stark, 1995; Karras, 1992).

When negotiating conflicts, the **Problem** is a completely different ball game and is referred to as the mediation **Process** where a third party comes into play. There are numerous authors on conflict resolution and mediation (Fisher, 1989, 1996; HBR, 2000; Pruitt, 1986; Stone, Patton and Heen, 2000; Susskind and Field, 1996; Ury, 1991, 2000).

The ability to accurately forecast the outcome of the negotiation is a function of how much knowledge and understanding one has of the external factors that affect one's industry and market. The P of **Prognosis** reminds us of the uncertainties that could make deals turn sour.

The P of **People** or **Players** is the main focus of this Appendix and is the most important P of all. After all, we are negotiating with people all the time, people with different business habits and cultures. So if we can get a better understanding of their issues, their business models and habits, we are more likely to achieve better results when we negotiate with them.

Some aspects of the P of **People** or **Players** that we focus upon here are the different cultures and their effect on the negotiation style. Let us define culture not only as the customs, institutions and achievements of a nation or peoples, but also as the corporate, professional and different communication behaviors and attitudes of peoples, including the role of gender.

The work developed by Dr. Jeswald Salacuse on culture and negotiation and the ten factors affecting the negotiation style, were studied and analyzed for people coming from Latin-American cultures, including different locations within Mexico, Ecuador and other countries in Latin America.

One trend of interest to international business people is that Latin-American and Mexican negotiators typically stand out for bringing creative elements to the negotiation table, while U.S. negotiators were typically found to bring a methodology and a plan for a win-win situation.

The analysis of the Latin-American culture's influence on negotiation within the context of the Chamoun model (Diagram II.4) has enabled construction of useful profiles for different business sectors. While nothing replaces relationship building on an individual basis, every person doing business with Latin Americans will benefit from this cross-section of expectations and preferences in business negotiating. Every individual has a unique negotiating style. This style is a product of childhood upbringing, family environment, professional and business experience, culture and other life experiences.

Allow me to offer you one further word of caution before continuing with our discussion on negotiations. A small percentage of people are, by nature, opposed to constructive negotiations. They are easy to spot when they are openly critical to you. Sometimes their influence can be neutralized through recognition of the organization's chain-of-command structure. What can be devastating to your negotiations is when they are covert. When covert, they give the appearance of being friendly and helpful when in reality they are working behind the scenes to sabotage the negotiations. These people, whether covert or not, must be removed from impacting the negotiations. Otherwise, you are totally wasting your time and energy.

Over the last 10 years, negotiation as a methodological practice, has received greater attention as business has become more complicated, increasingly global, more competitive and better informed.

A recent investigation carried out by Dr. Habib Chamoun-Nicolas sought to provide a better understanding of the way Mexicans and Latin Americans negotiate. The investigation carried out a survey of some 600 local professionals of different gender, age groups, industrial sectors, and regions. The study is based on the negotiating model developed by Dr. Jeswald Salacuse, professor at Tufts University of Diplomacy, and reported in <u>Making Global Deals</u> and the <u>Program on Negotiation</u> at Harvard. The following are some of the study's most notable findings and recommendations on how to negotiate in Mexico and Latin America.

First, let us introduce a summary of the ten factors that affect the negotiation style, highlighting the findings. To have a more in-depth description of the factors, see <u>Making Global Deals</u> by Dr. Jeswald Salacuse.

Contract versus Relationship

Are negotiations commonly conducted with the aim of signing a one-time contract, or establishing a long-term relationship?

Not surprisingly, lawyers are the ones who focus the most on individual contracts, with over 70% of those interviewed favoring this option.

Bureaucrats rank in at 60%, while 43% of surveys in scientific or technological professions favored this negotiating style. By comparison, just 32% of female executives preferred one-time contract negotiating and placed more importance on establishing long-term relationships.

Traditionally, the Latin-American culture favors building long-term relationships over the specific contracts. At present, urban and more economically dynamic areas in Mexico give contracts more importance than relationships due to their exposure to foreign cultures, global corporations and the implicit risks of investing higher levels of resources. However, there are still many parts of Mexico and Latin America where a firm handshake means more than a written contract.

Dr. Salacuse's work suggests Mexicans favor contracts (42%) less than Americans (54%) (Salacuse, 1998).

Negotiating Attitude: Zero-sum?

In a win-win scenario, both sides attempt to reach objectives for a mutually beneficial agreement. A zero-sum (win-lose) situation demands that one of the two parties concede significant aspects for the sake of reaching the agreement.

The investigations showed that more than 80% of the Mexicans and a 65% of Latin Americans have a win-win attitude when it comes to negotiating. The remaining sees negotiation as zero-sum.

This is often the case with bureaucrats, with 55% of them approaching negotiations as a win-lose situation.

The study also detected that in some cases losing a negotiation is not important, providing that the other party doesn't win.

According to Dr. Salacuse, 50% of Mexicans favor win-win (50%), versus 71% of Americans (Salacuse, 1998).

Attitude: Formal or Informal?

A formal negotiator will address other participants by their professional titles and avoid dealing on a close or personal level. The informal negotiator seeks a friendlier, more personal relationship and attempts to create a casual and more comfortable environment.

Fifty five percent of Mexican professionals in science and technology showed preference for informal negotiations, opposed to 43% of female executives. The negotiating culture tends to be more informal among small and medium-sized businesses. Sixty two percent of bureaucrats favored formality.

Dr. Salacuse's research results show that 58% of Mexicans participating in this survey tend to conduct informal negotiations, and that this tendency is 83% for Americans (Salacuse, 1998).

Communication: Direct or Indirect?

Direct communication makes use of straightforward and simple phrases to describe a situation. Indirect communication assumes that the other party has a significantly high level of education and/or understanding, which enables the use of insinuations, hints, and veiled remarks to express an opinion or a decision.

Some 89.5% of female executives preferred direct dealing, as did 80% of bureaucrats and 75% of those in scientific or technological professions. Only 30% of those with administrative functions preferred a direct style.

Dr. Salacuse reported that Mexicans participating in the survey had a tendency to prefer direct communication (100%) and 95% of the Americans also did (Salacuse, 1998). It is important to note that the organizational culture of the participants as well as their international experience may have influenced their responses to the survey.

Time Sensitivity: High or Low?

High sensitivity reflects a strong interest in punctuality and formality. Low sensitivity indicates greater flexibility in schedules and less punctuality in appointments.

The study indicated that those most sensitive to time were those in science-related professions, at 82%, followed by female executives, at 75%. Seventy percent of lawyers were sensitive to time. Only 56% of bureaucrats were highly sensitive to punctuality.

Time sensitivity was found to vary substantially depending on the geographic region in Mexico and Ecuador. For example, Mexico City, Guadalajara, Monterrey and Quito prove to be far more time sensitive than cities such as Merida, Veracruz and Guayaquil.

Dr. Salacuse's research results showed that Mexicans participating in the survey had a lower sensitivity to time (33%), similar to Americans (15%) (Salacuse,1998).

Emotional Display: High or Low

Some negotiators may hide or play down their emotions, while others do not hesitate to demonstrate their emotions when negotiating.

Some 86% of female executives demonstrated high sensitivity to emotions. On the other hand, just 30% of directors of small and medium-sized firms were emotionally sensitive.

Dr. Salacuse reports that Mexicans participating in the survey had a tendency toward high emotional sensitivity (83%), slightly higher than Americans (74%). (Salacuse, 1998)

Agreements: General or Specific?

A specific agreement refers to a detailed listing of all aspects related to the deal. General contracts do not usually cover all the specifics and are intentionally left open in order to continue the relationship.

Among Mexican and Latin-American respondents, female executives (70%), lawyers (90%) and bureaucrats (90%) said they prefer to be specific when negotiating. On the other hand, directors of small and medium-sized firms (70%) said they prefer to negotiate in general terms.

Dr. Salacuse's research results shows that Mexicans participating in the survey had a tendency for more specific agreements (83%) than the Americans did (78%) (see Salacuse, J. *Ten Ways that Culture Affects Negotiating Style: Some Survey Results*. Negotiation Journal. July 1998).

Building An Agreement: Bottom Up or Top Down?

This refers to the form in which the agreement is built. Whether the agreement process starts from agreeing to specific terms and then builds to a general contract (bottom-up) or whether it starts from general terms and proceeds to specific ones (top-down).

Amongst our study group, female executives (59%), lawyers (65%), and bureaucrats (75%) said they prefer to build agreements bottom-up. On the other hand, directors of small and medium-sized firms (70%) prefer negotiating from general terms to specifics.

Dr. Salacuse's research results show that both Mexicans (67%) and Americans (53%) had a tendency to build agreements from the bottom-up (Salacuse, 1998).

Team Management: Leadership or Consensus?

In some groups, management can make negotiation decisions on their own. In other organizations, decisions are made only after consulting team players. While female executives and lawyers show a slight preference for decisions by one leader (55%), the survey found that most prefer to reach decisions through consensus.

Research results shows that Mexicans participating in the survey had a tendency to conduct the negotiation with one leader (91%), considerably more so than Americans (63%)(Salacuse, 1998)

Even though Mexicans are perceived as preferring one leader conducting the negotiation, most Mexicans have a tendency to consult their families, friends, and coworkers before going to a final decision making process.

Risk Tolerance: High or Low?

Some negotiators are likely to run greater risks when doing business, exposing themselves to higher degrees of uncertainty. By comparison, those inclined to low-risk business styles avoid complications that could arise before closing any deal.

In our survey, female executives and directors of small and medium-sized businesses demonstrated a 72 % capacity to take risks. The lowest reported risk takers were bureaucrats, at just 48%.

Dr. Salacuse reported that Americans showed a tendency to take risks (78%), while Mexicans, on the other hand, were evenly divided between risk takers and conservative negotiators. Mexican women registered higher percentages of risk taking than men from the same culture (i.e., Mexican men (44%), Mexican women (67%)) (Salacuse, 1998).

Mexican Survey Profiles:

Young male executives and professionals

These have tough negotiating and decision-making styles based on logical grounds. They are easier to convince with data that provides evidence of tangible medium and long-term benefits for their organization. They seek win-win situations, are more focused on contracts than relationships and are more likely to favor negotiating in general terms over specifics.

Young female executives and professionals

These make decisions slowly and cautiously and need to have all the angles covered before reaching an agreement. Their negotiating style focuses more on the specifics than on generalities. They are detail oriented, and while contracts are important, the relationship is even more so.

Executives older than 50 without a university degree

These are tough negotiators who are more interested in the relationship than in the contract. They make decisions based on impulses, and later, justify them logically.

Different geographic areas

In Central and Southern Mexico, relationships are considered more important than contracts, and businesspeople are more indirect in their negotiating style. In Northern Mexico, businesspeople tend to favor contracts and a more direct negotiating style.

Among the research findings, certain tendencies were noted that explain some of the enigmas of the Latin-American style of negotiation.

We believe that the Latin-American Style of negotiators is the prototype of a creative negotiator.

Let us take a closer look at Mexico as the leading country of Latin America to see if we can discover what is going on.

A very interesting negotiation phenomenon has taken place in Mexico during this past decade. The Mexican people are shifting from a zero-sum mindset to a global vision negotiation mindset. The open market in Mexico and in the rest of the world is forcing the old-style zero-sum negotiation to be more focused on a win-win negotiation outcome.

People start thinking win/win scenarios when coming into a day-to-day negotiation process. Mexico's new negotiation style is the result of striving for business independence and intellectual freedom. The trend to better educate and empower people to negotiate will mitigate corruption in the future.

The Mexican and Latinamerican overall negotiation style has the characteristic of a continuous struggle for survival, showing many persuasive and manipulative skills.

Not only have great changes happened in Mexico with the open market economy, but also in the political arena. The ruling political party (PRI), after more than 70 years in power, lost the administration to the opposition party (PAN). This change took place without a revolution or insurrection. This is also an indication that Mexicans are tired of "business as usual" and that a forward-thinking and better prepared society is arising. This change in behavior of voting versus being indifferent to the vote is seen as an indicator that Mexicans are not only fighting for their political rights, but doing so in an orderly manner. This is also reflected in the negotiation tendencies as well. Mexican people in the past either were simply too afraid to ask or were thought unreasonable for what they were asking. Now the tendency is to ask when there is a basis for their case. The successful Mexican businessperson is now preparing himself with plans and strategies and the understanding of other cultures, in order to achieve better global **Deals.**

One should picture the Mexican and Latin-American negotiation style as a very creative negotiation style, including the invention of options. Inventing options increases the negotiation scenarios for the parties. The pitfall is that people don't show their interest behind the negotiation position very easily, and those who do show their interest, are at risk of being taking advantage of. Another pitfall is that, even though time sensitivity is not very high according to the research, Mexican people tend to go though the negotiation quickly and look for a very high return on investment. In doing so, a lot of value is left on the negotiating table and both parties lose in the long term.

Among the questions that come to mind are:
- Is the Latin-American negotiation style a unique one?
- What are the unique characteristics of negotiating with Latin Americans?

Is there a culture of negotiation in Latin America?

Some of the typical negotiation behaviors and tendencies observed in our sample of more than 600 professionals, from different gender, professions and occupations are:

- An urgency or tendency to rush to close a deal,
- The "Mexican Standoff" approach to a non-negotiating agreement. (After many conversations and sales calls, the client disappears for a while without saying anything.),
- Some people prefer to lose the **Deal**, so long as the other party doesn't win either,
- A tendency to change the negotiation style according to the culture they are negotiating with,
- A tendency to be polite that leads to not saying NO, but not saying YES either,
- Some people show that they are afraid to make requests or ask questions.

In the past, to do business in Mexico, you didn't need to have a well-organized plan. You only needed to identify the opportunity and chase after it. Today, not only do you need to identify a business opportunity, but you also need to have a complete understanding and knowledge of competitors, customer needs, aspirations, desires, and the market. You also need to understand your strengths and weaknesses as perceived by your Mexican client before you sit down at the negotiating table.

The good news is that the differences in doing business between Mexico and the USA are becoming smaller as time goes by. Nevertheless, there is still a need for a sponsor or partner in Mexico or Latin America. It is just as important to have the right match (**the person**) as it is the right business (**the opportunity**).

That would be ideal. However, we need to do as the "Romans in Rome", but with the caveat "without compromising our values". One has to remember that values are the most difficult to negotiate among cultures, behaviors and attitudes are the least difficult, and in the middle between these two extremes, are norms and laws (Salacuse, 2000).

Understanding what behaviors and attitudes are negotiable is important as you begin the negotiation with another culture. We need to do more of our homework. If for instance, we are having lunch for the first time with a Mexico City client in a nice restaurant with a relaxed atmosphere, let the relationship develop. Don't get your yellow notebook out and write your business notes and facts at the table. It is considered inappropriate business behavior in Mexico, under the given circumstances. A more appropriate business behavior will be to develop a relationship, break the ice, and then go into business at a different location or at the end of the meal.

Even though, according to our research, Mexico is slowly being transformed from a relationship business society to a contract-oriented one, some places exist in Mexico where a handshake is worth more that a sealed contract. There are places where it is considered offensive to talk about business right away. Northern Mexico is the most direct and business-oriented community, while the Central and Southern parts are more relationship oriented. Large Mexican cities like Guadalajara, Mexico City and Monterrey are shifting to be more contract-oriented vs. being relationship-oriented. However, the relationship is still more important than a signed contract.

Watch out for stereotypes. One has to be aware that these findings do not apply to every business situation. We are presenting only tendencies that we have observed throughout Mexico and Latin-American countries. Mexico has 32 states, each of them with a very rich culture and which therefore, are very different from each other.

You could be having a 30 minute breakfast meeting in Monterrey and a 3 hour lunch in Mexico City, and be very effective businesswise in both cases. If you think you need a long lunch meeting in Monterrey to close a business successfully, you may be surprised. Different people from different Mexican cities have distinct business behaviors and attitudes. If you have to sit for long hours in a client's office to reach an agreement, be prepared to do so. Not every place has the same sense of urgency. The key in negotiating with other cultures is to understand them, tolerate them respectfully and above all, display patience with the timing differences.

You have to do your homework and understand what drives the Mexican and Latin-American client. For instance, in Monterrey, clients are more interested in having lunch with their families and friends, than with service providers. In Mexico City, distances are so great that a lot of business issues are discussed at long lunches. In Guadalajara, business is discussed on golf courses and is similar to Mexico City. Generally speaking, in Mexico City and Guadalajara, tradition is more important than business, and in Monterrey, business is more important than tradition.

The moral of this story is that understanding your client's background and his likes and dislikes will make your business ventures in Mexico, or anywhere else in Latin America, more enjoyable and more profitable for all parties.

As a rule of thumb, if you are dealing for the first time with a Mexican or Latin-American client, listen to his needs and wants and try to understand where he is coming from. Before you sell anything, spend some time and resources understanding the culture.

It is important to remember that if you are selling, you have to adapt to the culture you are selling to.

Do as your clients in their country without compromising your values ("When in Rome do as the Romans do" without compromising your values)

Some Suggestions for Non-Latin-Americans When Negotiating with Latin-Americans.

A common tendency for non-Mexican and non-Latin-American people is to assume that negotiating in Mexico and Latin America is the same as in their countries. You will be surprised at the misunderstandings that arise because of the cultural differences.

For example, if a client is requesting more information on your products and services, you may think that he is almost ready to make a buying decision. If you press him and he is not ready to make a final decision, the client will simply say, "NO! Not this time!" And that will be the end of the story.

Doing business in Mexico or Latin America can be a completely different ball game. The Mexican and Latin-American client, after requesting information for several months on your products or services, may suddenly stop communicating. This is the famous Mexican Stand Off. The client won't say, "NO! Not interested!" He will simply stop communicating, in order to avoid having to give you a negative response.

This is a common denominator with many Mexican and Latin-American clients. Instead of telling you NO as a straight answer, they avoid it and disappear for a while. What can you do? You have to be honest and direct and help them to tell you what it takes to change the NO! into a YES!

Closing the communication loop is a common problem for a lot of businesspeople in Mexico and Latin America. If you have a client in Mexico or Latin America and you send them an e-mail, ask them if they got it. An e-mail is not generally the best way to communicate. To establish business communication by telephone is more personal, but nothing replaces a face-to-face meeting.

Closing the cycle could be as simple as requesting that your Mexican or Latin-American partner reply to your e-mail. Sometimes Mexicans or Latin Americans wait to develop the best answer to your request on an e-mail, and it may take a long time to do so. If you want to accelerate the business closing, you need to be proactive and persistent.

Decision-makers in Mexico and Latin America are another factor affecting the negotiation style. Perception is everything in the sales and negotiation process. Don't always assume that the male is the one behind the decision. There could be a female that influences the decision process who may not even appear on the organizational chart of the client company (or vice-versa).

Persistence is important to close deals, but it has been our experience that repetitively calling a client in Mexico or Latin America could have the opposite effect. Then, the client ignores us and doesn't return our calls or e-mails. Be honest, up front and direct.

Ask probing questions like:

>Are you really interested in our services?
>Is this only to have an order of magnitude of the cost?
>If it is urgent, why is it so?
>Are you ready to make a purchasing decision?
>What is the buying process?

What are your basic needs?
How do you know that my services fulfill your needs?
What are your expectations?
What are your aspirations?

Sales Pipeline in Latin America

Filling the sales pipeline or funnel with a Mexican or Latin-American client is not a straight shot like in the USA, and we need to adjust to cultural behaviors.

Based on the fact that Mexican and Latin-American businesses are heavily dependent on a "relationship first" basis, try to avoid the common beginner's mistakes of forcing fake empathy. Appearing to be friendly to a Mexican or Latin American client is worse than being direct and sincere, so be yourself.

While prospecting a new client, it is best to be indirect, and less confrontational while asking more open type of questions. At the closing stage, it is more effective to be direct, assertive and to the point.

It always works at the closing stage to ask the Mexican or Latin-American client, what in his mind it would take to get to a YES! The client, having developed a relationship with you, will be more realistic about his demands to make a deal happen.

Common Frustrations

You may have experienced frustration when negotiating in Mexico or Latin America because of the following:

Your clients:
- Don't answer e-mails or phone calls,
- Give you "tomorrow" as an answer,

- Don't pay you the overdue bills,
- Don't give you NO! as an answer, but a YES! instead and still, nothing is happening,
- After a continuum of interactions, all of the sudden, they don't talk to you,
- Are the wrong decision makers.

Suggestions to avoid or minimize frustrations

The solution to avoid some of the above mentioned common business practices all over the world are:

- Do your homework and know who you are dealing with-(Decision makers and influencers, track record),
- Use ultimatum tactics after investment of resources from both parties,
- Help the client, step by step, to reach agreement,
- Be honest and ask them straight out why they are requesting all the information,
- Invite the client to visit your office in your country- (If they are willing to invest, that means they are serious.),
- Don't give more information, until they give some thing in return,
- Set up limits and business rules-(Do's and don'ts),
- Don't set precedents,
- Insist for a written agreement to better understand what to expect from each other,
- Ask for a down payment and a payment schedule.

The ultimatum is a good tool to **Deal** with a Mexican and Latin-American client that is undecided and has spent a lot of your time and resources. It helps force the client to make a decision.

Be straight and to the point with the client.

As a general rule of thumb, you should ask for a down payment or a payment schedule as part of the negotiation items before you deliver any work, to avoid late payments or no payments at all.

Control yourself and your feelings

In an extreme case where a client keeps you waiting three hours on the first visit to their office, be prepared to do other work while waiting. Don't lose your patience, because you will lose the business AND your patience. Being late to a meeting doesn't mean they don't care. Maybe more important things came up at the last minute. If you have a bad reaction, you will lose all the effort that you put in the sales call. Ego is a Cancer for business.

Doing business with another culture starts with understanding our culture and theirs

We have discovered that, in general Mexican and Latin-American small and medium businesses don't have a well established sales and negotiation methodology, a business plan or any formal strategic planning process. They are very creative and apply creativity in doing business. Because of improvements in the global business environment in Mexico during the past decade, Mexican businesspeople have realized the importance of planning and have been dramatically changing from a non-planning society to one of planning with creativity.

A win-win situation for non-Mexicans and non-Latin Americans is the following: As a foreign partner you should help your Mexican or Latin-American partners in becoming more organized and to better plan their business activities and goals.

In return, your Mexican and Latin-American partners will contribute creativity and know-how to your business.

The old stereotype of doing business in Mexico with Mexican businesspeople being late for appointments and not caring is fading away.

A.2 The Argentinean Style of Negotiation by Pablo M. Linzoain

In this Appendix, we present *The Argentinean Style of Negotiation* by Pablo M. Linzoain. We found many similarities between this study and that of the author which refers to the Mexican style of negotiation (Book, "Business Development. 3rd edition). It is not our intention to create stereotypes or make general assumptions. Statistical rigor has not been applied to the results of this research. The results simply present typical tendencies. When a Mexican or a Latin American faces a foreign culture, he "becomes smaller" (Ramírez, 2002), as if the other culture was intimidating, causing him to lose power of negotiation. On the other hand, when an Argentinean faces another culture with a lot of pride, such as the Americans, their pride, and not intimidation, comes to the forefront. What in the beginning might seem to give him power in the negotiation will cause him to lose **Power** if he persists. These samples intend to help us understand our counterparts by giving insight to their way of thinking, and enabling us to achieve win-win negotiations.

Before discussing the characteristics of the Argentinean negotiator, it is important to point out that this research project sought to identify the *typical* or *most common* traits in Argentinean management's negotiating style. It should be clear that not everyone in Argentina possesses the same attributes. Also, the author is aware of the valuable advice given by Breslin (1989):

Stereotyping is often done unconsciously, and it becomes an ingrained, unnoticed practice. Breslin also accurately stated that if groups of different cultures learn more about one another, assumptions — particularly negative ones — will have less of an influence on their final decisions.

Moreover, according to Graham and Cateora (1999), it should be clearly understood that individual personalities and backgrounds heavily influence behaviour at the negotiation table and it is the manager's responsibility to consider these factors. Also, different people have different objectives, interests and forms of communication, according to Fisher *et al* (1991). Therefore, different things may be persuasive to them, and they may have different ways of making decisions. For the purpose of this research paper, the definition of culture comes from Salacuse (1998), who said culture is the socially transmitted behavior patterns, norms, beliefs and values of a given community.

To have a better understanding of Argentinean executives, it is important to understand Argentineans in general. Roman Catholicism is the official religion of Argentina, with approximately 90 percent of the population practising this religion. Judaism accounts for 2 percent, and other religions account for 8 percent. Freedom of religion is guaranteed. Eighty-five percent of the population is white and the literacy rate is 95 percent. The official language is Spanish.

Though Argentina is a country with people of varied ancestry, it is probably the most European country of South and Central America. In the late 19th and early 20th centuries, Argentina attracted many immigrants from Europe. Around 1920, one-third of the country's population was foreign-born, predominantly Italians and Spaniards. There were also Russians, Polish, French, Turks, Lebanese and Syrians. In 1998, the population was 36,125,000, with approximately 85 percent being of

European descent. Two executives interviewed at separate times for the research project agreed on the same point: *"Argentineans are a bit of everything; Spanish, Turkish, Syrian, Italian, German, French, etc."* This diversity leads to a mix of behavioural styles at the negotiation table. (Some executives joked that *"Argentineans bargain as Arabs, shout as Italians, exaggerate as Spaniards, and demand as Germans."*)

Team organization: one leader or group consensus?

According to Salacuse (1998), in any international negotiation it is vital to understand the way groups are organized and the way organizations function. He said that one extreme is a negotiation team with a supreme leader who has complete authority to decide; the other extreme are cultures that stress team and decision-making by consensus. The majority of the Argentinean individuals interviewed admitted preferring to have complete authority. However, depending on what the circumstances dictate, either method might be used.

Most of the executives interviewed preferred to go to the negotiation table alone, and then return to their companies and personally explain the outcome of the negotiation to their co-workers. More than 70 percent of the executives considered it better to meet their counterpart alone, regardless of how many individuals were with the counterpart. In contrast, the usual tendency in international negotiation is to go in as a group because they value discussing each person's opinion after the negotiation. It is appropriate to remember that Argentina is a country with limited experience in the arena of international markets. Consequently, small and medium-sized companies demonstrate a degree of inexperience in cross-culture transactions.

The principal reasons identified during the interviews supporting:

The Preference To Go Alone Are:

- To be comfortable and free to express themselves with out having to confer with their partners.
- To go to see what happens, what the counterpart demands and offers.
- To protect the information managed by each area of the company because its disclosure constitutes a loss of power.
- To accelerate the negotiation process.
- To observe whether or not there is an opportunity to build a good relationship with the counterpart.

The Preference To Go With A Team Are:

- Need for advice from other professionals, such as lawyers, economists or engineers, who could provide the negotiators with relevant information when needed.
- Need input from technical or administrative specialists with specific expertise in their respective fields-(accountants, payroll or credit clearance administrators, etc. But they are not part of the negotiation process),
- Desire to play a game in which one negotiator seems to be on the side of the counterpart while the other one seems to be opposing him/her-(By using this technique, it is sometimes possible to achieve the goals of the negotiation faster than in using traditional negotiation methods.)
- Desire to increase the confidence of the primary negotiator. Also, it is important that the people on the negotiation team have confidence in one another.

Other findings: One issue supporting the decision to negotiate alone arises from the need to avoid disclosing ideas to the other party.

In addition, the interviews reveal that Argentineans generally do not prepare themselves for the negotiations in advance. This may be due to the fact that Argentineans regard themselves as possessing a high degree of self-confidence, creativity and ability to improvise when facing uncertain situations. Very few executives demonstrated an interest in teams working towards the goals and means of the negotiation. The Argentinean executives do not have a high regard for the benefits of negotiating with a team.

The idea of including young executives in the negotiations is popular *in theory*. However, it is difficult to achieve due to several issues. Fears about interference with the negotiation, leaks of information, high personnel turnover in medium-level management, and the difficulty in teaching the young people the company's way of negotiation are the main issues put forward by the interviewees. For example, one of the executives confessed to learning negotiating skills by observing his boss during negotiations. He recalls what his boss told him once, *"Look at what we do and the way we do It because I cannot teach you. You will learn by observing me."* In addition, human resources are usually scarce in many small- and medium-sized companies.

Personal style: informal vs formal?

In Argentina there is a tendency to start a negotiation in a formal manner. This includes addressing the counterpart by his academic title or surname — so that proper respect can be demonstrated. (Argentineans consider it being respectful to use the other negotiator's academic title.) Furthermore, studies by Volkema and Chang (1998), on Latin America showed that initial encounters are likely to begin with formal communications, including the use of academic titles and formal credentials, as well as the exchanging of calling cards. It has also been stated that only a very high-level executive could begin a negotiation in an informal way, without previous acknowledgement of his counterpart.

Nevertheless, all of the respondents demonstrated the intention to build confidence between the two sides by using a degree of informality that helps develop a more comfortable level of communication. It is a common practice to begin the meeting with comments about football, politics or the economy without expressing a particular opinion. These comments are used to ascertain the opinion and points of view of the counterpart. (One entrepreneur argued that "*Argentineans talk about politics and sports and that this waste of time can be fruitfully used for the negotiation.*" He also added, *"In general, their time management is not so good."*) Jokes and funny stories are also a good way to set an informal tone and help generate an environment of mutual confidence.

In Argentina there is a common belief that to build a strong foundation for a successful negotiation relationship, one must go from a formal approach to negotiating to an informal one and not the other way around. This is why, despite showing a preference towards conducting the negotiation in an informal environment, most of the respondents reiterated the importance of starting the business relationship on a formal and respectful basis.

According to the interviewees, some of the reasons supporting informality in the negotiations are:

- There exists a higher level of sincerity between people,
- The communication becomes warmer and more fluent,
- A comfort level is achieved that makes it difficult for confrontation,
- Increased confidence and friendliness with the counterpart.

Negotiators need to project a professional image. This means wearing an elegant suit, necktie, well-shined shoes, etc. In many cases, very informal outfits may be interpreted as a lack of interest in the negotiation. For Argentinean negotiators, first impressions are important and demonstrations of appropriate respect are crucial.

There is a distinct difference between the residents of Capital Federal (Buenos Aires), who are known as "Porteños" ("people of the port"), and the representatives of the rest of the country. This is due to the fact that the "Porteños" often develop confidence with the other part more quickly. For instance, they use the less formal word "vos" instead of the more formal "tu" (both words mean "you") to give a sense of informality. People from outside Buenos Aires often accuse "Porteños" of having an air of superiority over people from other parts of the country.

Argentineans' punctuality and written memoranda are somewhat more informal than in the U.S., though it does seem to be more formal than other South American countries. For an Argentinean businessman to arrive five to 10 minutes late for a meeting does not create a bad impression. However, most German executives do not tolerate this behaviour (Slate Emily, 1994).

The majority of the interviewees agreed that Americans go straight to the heart of the negotiation's issues and express themselves clearly. However, they face difficulties and demonstrate a certain degree of discomfort when having to bargain for prices with Arabic businessmen. According to Salacuse (1998), Americans are quick to make a deal, while Germans are slow to negotiate and make decisions, but Germans are always punctual. Argentinean executives are moderate in terms of the time needed to make a deal (not quick but not too slow), but less concerned about punctuality than Germans.

Argentinean executives believe a serious tone is important to prevent wasting valuable time and to get to the central issues of the negotiation. One executive asserted "*Setting a serious tone is important in order to not waste time, though we must go on with the friendship and politeness between the parties.*" This comment clearly shows that seriousness does not preclude friendship and politeness. In this regard, Argentinean interviewees accused their Bolivian and Paraguayan counterparts of being too bureaucratic. However, Argentineans have more positive working relationships with Mexican businessmen.

In conclusion, some of the key features favoured by many Argentinean executives are informality in the negotiation relationship, friendship, the possibility to develop more than just a business relationship, and the ability to share goals and ideas. One must be able to start a negotiation in a formal manner and quickly make an effortless transition to achieve an informal environment. In general, the negotiation will hopefully develop into a comfortable working atmosphere. That makes sense because Latin-American negotiators may be more willing to share information with someone who is perceived to be a friend rather than a stranger (Volkema and Chang, 1998). It is important to stress the strong influence of the North American literature on the Argentinean business community mainly through popular business books that have been translated into Spanish. Examples of such books are "Getting To Yes", by Fisher, Ury and Patton, and "The Art And Science Of Negotiation" by H. Raiffa, among others.

Stereotypes

In general, executives believe stereotypes that they have heard from colleagues or that they have learned from experience. One famous stereotype is "John Wayne," which represents the cowboy-like American negotiating style of "*shoot first; ask questions later.*" The "samurai," who is a fierce warrior, represents the Japanese negotiator. It should be noted that in Argentina there exists a weak tendency to study cultural stereotypes due to the lack of Spanish bibliography. However, all the interviewers expressed a great enthusiasm for reading this kind of information. They also affirmed having interest in the history and customs of the counterpart's homeland.

However, approximately half of the executives confessed that they do little research on the counterpart's customs and culture. Moreover, any research about stereotypes is generally done during the negotiation period. According to one of the executives, one of the reasons for the lack of research is that there are not many opportunities for long-term projects in Argentina.

Executives believe that Americans are the most precise and clearest negotiators. Americans, as well as Germans, are clearly identified as being very professional, but the latter are criticised for being less flexible and less open to the changes required by the Argentinean market. In regards to their fellow South Americans, they said they experience a lower level of stress in negotiations due to the similarity in language, religion and history (the colonization and independence of these nations produced similar historical frameworks). The point here is that culture, history, language, values, decision-making processes and institutions often have enormous impact in the negotiations. However, the negotiations are conducted by people and not between national stereotypes. Graham and Cateora (1999) say companies and countries do not negotiate, people do.

Argentineans feel proud of their country and they generally have a strong sense of national pride at home and abroad. Occasionally, when one demonstrates knowledge about Argentinean culture and history, and not only about football, agriculture and meat, one is better able to gain an executive's trust. This is one of the reasons why Spain maintains strong lobbies in several sections of the Argentinean economy. Spaniards understand the Argentineans quite well. This is one of the reasons why Spain is called Argentina's Motherland.

Foreign languages

For most executives, English is the language of business. More than 70 percent of the executives interviewed understand the English language, but only 30 percent feel confident speaking English while negotiating.

The remaining executives prefer to use translators, and the reasons they gave were:

- To have more time to think in the negotiation,
- To not spend time thinking in the language, but to use that time to get to know the counterpart better,
- To properly express their thoughts and opinions.

Some problems arise when considering the participation of interpreters. It is necessary to talk with the interpreters before negotiations begin, especially when the translator is a native to another Spanish speaking country. Mexicans, for example, use expressions that are difficult for Argentineans to understand and visa versa. This difficult situation frequently hinders good communication.

Another problem is that when the translator is a member of the company's staff, he/she can misunderstand his/her role in the negotiation. Because the translator knows the business and the language in which the negotiation is being performed, it may give him/her a feeling of self-confidence that causes the translator to go beyond what the group leader intended. The translator may inject personal ideas into the negotiation. This is another difficulty that may arise in a team negotiation.

Stages for negotiation of international businesses

Graham and Herberger Jr. (1983) suggest four stages for international negotiation: First, non-task communication that provides information to the two parties without discussing the negotiation issues. Second, an exchange of task-related information. Third, persuasion. Finally, concessions and agreement (see Diagram V.7).

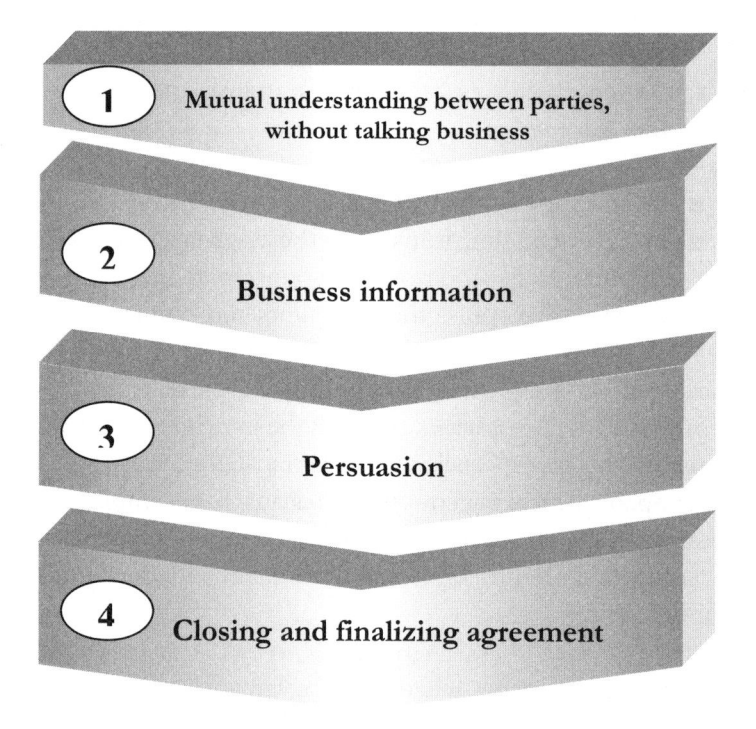

1. Mutual understanding between parties, without talking business
2. Business information
3. Persuasion
4. Closing and finalizing agreement

Diagram V.7 Stages in International Negotiation, according to Graham and Herberger, 1983

For the Argentineans, persuasion is the most important stage. More than 70 percent of those interviewed talked about spending most of the time persuading the other side. They see it as the art of seduction. One of the businessmen interviewed emphasised that *"to be efficient in persuasion, one must be well prepared/trained, know precisely what is wanted and have personal conviction."* According to the chairman of an important trade company, during this third stage *"We will use the ace we have up our sleeve."* It is clear now that this stage will begin when the parties trust each other.

Identification of the counterpart's interests becomes one of the most important points that must be observed. Therefore, one should be alert. One of the managers, who has dealt with negotiations in the last five years for sums of up to $800 million dollars, said; *"I try to identify what the counterpart wants in order to persuade him/her in a better way, and many times I have to help him to understand what he is really seeking."*

However, the second stage, which is the exchange of task-related information, requires more attention at the start of the negotiation. This stage will be regarded as the most important from this point forward. When companies meet for the first time, they must pay special attention to this stage the presenting the company, and the terms, as well as conditions of the possible business. One executive said, *"They proceed in a roundabout way before a clear depiction of the business is made."* Moreover, they agreed that this comes from a lack of preparation.

How should the cards be displayed?

More than 85 percent of those interviewed admitted that it is not advantageous to show all their cards at the beginning of the negotiation. This will happen through a process, which establishes that as long as the counterpart shows his/her cards, they will show their cards. An example of an Argentinean negotiator's inexperience occurred on a trip to an Arab country on which he commented, *"I showed all the terms and conditions and I was very sincere from the beginning."* As a result of this error in the strategy, he confronted the strong bargaining tactics of the Arabs, who wanted to obtain something more. This led to a breakdown of the business negotiation. He was not able to show better conditions than the one he had shown at the beginning. This businessman concluded: *"Now I show only what is absolutely necessary during any part of the negotiation."* Many Argentinean businessmen have made the mistake of showing everything too soon and of trying to reach a quick agreement. The root of the problem is their insufficient experience in international negotiations because the Argentinean economy has only recently opened up to international markets.

All those interviewed agreed on the fact that it is of vital importance to have an ace up your sleeve, and secondly, it should only be used when absolutely necessary. They said that is very difficult for them to have an ace when conducting negotiations in the global market. A businessman affirmed: *"This is difficult because we are not as competitive in these new global markets as we would like to be."*

Information is an essential component of the negotiation. Argentina has experienced many changes and has had to quickly adapt to new circumstances with limited financial resources. Thus, an excellent negotiator is seen as a person able to produce new ideas and options, and even to create an ace during the negotiation. According to one entrepreneur, *"Negotiation is not a straight line. It has to be imaginative and innovative, defining the conversation so as to make the other party see the whole situation. You should make the topic interesting in order to seduce the other party."* All of that has contributed to fostering a very innovative and creative Argentinean negotiation style.

Afraid of severing the relationship or betraying the counterpart's trust, the businessman will not only hide the ace until the end of the negotiation, but he will proceed with the negotiation even after denying having authority for performing such a transaction. He may continue to negotiate even after alleging that it is a new situation and that he needs to consult with his/her executive officer on the change in circumstance.

A characteristic of Latin Americans, including Argentineans, is to speak using long statements that say nothing, trying to fill up spaces of silence. Most businessmen interviewed described the typical Argentinean as a very talkative person and, for that reason, somewhat impractical.

Negotiation goal: contract or relationship?

According to Graham and Herberger (1983), a signed contract does not have the same meaning in Tokyo, Rio or Riyadh as it does in New York. Different cultures view the very purpose of a business negotiation differently (Salacuse, 1998). Volkema and Chang (1998) established that many Latin Americans believe that it is an individual's word more than his or her signature that binds an agreement. In Argentina, a verbal agreement is more important than a signed contract, which is only drafted in cases where problems arise. However, the acceptance and intention of signing contracts is greater in international than in domestic negotiations. Compromise and words said during the negotiation are of greater value. Generally, flexibility is a characteristic of Argentinean businessmen.

Most of the managers agreed that they do not have any problem signing a contract, but that this is not their favorite task. They prefer to trust and have an excellent understanding of the situation, so as to never have to deal with a written contract. Contracts exist and they establish limitations and rights, though in general Argentineans consider it more important to know the quality of the company and its personnel. In many cases, businessmen stated that it is very important to be aware of the counterpart's background and the ethics of the company. In this way, Argentinean executives are unlike their American counterparts. According to Salacuse (1998), the goal of a negotiation for Americans is to arrive at a signed contract between parties. What is more, most of the interviewees believed in not writing very detailed contracts, stating that contracts only need to include the main ideas of the negotiation agreement. There is a pronounced difference between Buenos Aires and the rest of the country, since the latter group is more likely to negotiate verbally, whereas in Buenos Aires the concept of written contracts is becoming more common.

The research data showed that the executives possessed a clear inclination toward personal relationships, which play a central role in the negotiation process. An important statement, according to Ertel (1999), is that it is common for negotiators to confuse the deal and the relationship. This is an especially frequent problem for Argentinean negotiators. Both parties must trust each other in order to build a positive working relationship. However, sometimes in Argentina the concept of trust can be misunderstood because of the display of affection and camaraderie during the negotiation. Several executives point out that they sometimes misunderstand the counterpart due to the difficulty of recognizing the differences between friend, colleague and business relation. It may be difficult to establish the line between personal relationship and business relationship, and to be able to recognize that the deal does not always mean friendship between the two parties.

Considering other alternatives

Fisher, Ury, and Patton (1991) say that the reason for negotiating is to produce a better result than the one that may be obtained without a negotiation. So, before the negotiation, it is imperative to determine the point at which the negotiator will walk away from accepting any agreement with the other side.

Half the businessmen interviewed confirmed not pursuing alternatives to the main goal of the negotiation. There is often no predetermined decision to find other alternatives if the main goal isn't achieved. Argentinean businessmen are considered skilled at improvising, which results in little effort being spent on considering possible alternatives prior to the negotiation. Argentinean businessmen admitted to entering into numerous negotiations with little or no prior preparation, yet remaining optimistic about a successful agreement. (Argentineans are characterized as working progressively and persistently, instead of having a planned course of action.) However, according to Fisher *et al* (1991), having at least a tentative Best Alternative To a Negotiated Agreement – BATNA– (Fisher *et al*, 1991) is absolutely essential to conducting the negotiations wisely. Negotiators should always think through their alternatives before they even start to negotiate (Ertel, 1999).

Argentinean businessmen work in a domestic market whose population does not exceed 40 million. It's important to point out that it is a relatively small market and that means businesses often have few alternatives. There is a lot of acceptance of the status quo because the domestic market's size restricts the number of potential alternatives.

There is little enthusiasm to plan for long-term outcomes. The common focus is to react to and work on short-term objectives. Various businessmen affirmed *"It is very difficult to think of long-term results due to the abrupt changes in Argentina's economy and its brief time under democracy."* This leads to an acceptance of instability almost as a norm, which makes future planning practically impossible. That is why intuition and quick reaction are more commonly used than long-term planning.

One executive claimed that he explored his alternatives, seeking two points: First, to be able to pressure the counterpart in a way that brings closure to the agreement, and second, to demonstrate his understanding and awareness of the business. He acknowledged *"It is good to pretend to have an alternative B in the negotiation, despite the fact that B does not exist."* Furthermore, the negotiation process is occasionally perceived as a measurement of strength between parties.

Silences

Argentineans do not typically cope well with period of silence. More than 90 percent of the executives agreed that silences are uncomfortable. Argentineans feel that these moments should be quickly filled with conversation. One of the executives affirmed, *"Silences have to be used to make points, persuade, or express concepts."* Moreover, almost 80 percent considered that one should speak when the other party is quiet and use it as opportunity to provide more information.

According to Volkema and Chang (1998), many Latin Americans place a high value on verbal skills in negotiations, particularly the ability to respond quickly to another's claims or challenges. Argentinean negotiators usually give a spontaneous, quick answer and this is sometimes expressed in advance. There are people who believe that a quick response is better than a thoughtful one.

There are other cultures that believe in answering more carefully. One executive commented, *"We experience the mistake of answering in advance, and we should carefully consider our answers."* Due to what has been expressed and analyzed, it has been observed that Argentineans negotiate with strong emotions and find it difficult to stay calm.

Taking "no" as an answer

History shows that Argentineans had to fight to achieve their independence during the period of 1810-1820. They struggled and fought to receive dignified wages during the 1940s under President Peron's leadership and are currently struggling to maintain their economy and young democracy. All this reflects a tenacious people and reveals an optimistic spirit that other nations would not consider possible, given the present economic circumstances in Argentina.

All of those interviewed agreed on the principle of accepting "no" only as a temporary answer. A common characteristic displayed by Argentinean negotiators is a high level of persistence. They are extremely optimistic and persistent. Some businessmen defined themselves as positive and unwilling to give up after hearing "no" for the first time. An important point to highlight is the lack of alternatives with other companies. As previously mentioned, there is not a large market and this leads to a relentless persistence.

Since it is difficult to find many other companies with which to do business, one will try to maintain negotiations with the first contact. One businessman affirmed, *"As this is a tiny market, and there are few alternatives to establish new businesses, we will keep working with the few options available to us."* This is why when there is a possible new business opportunity, persistence becomes the most valued attribute of the Argentinean executive. On the contrary, in other countries, such as Germany, if an agreement is not reached, businesses have many alternatives with other companies.

Many of the Argentineans interviewed admitted that preparation is their weak point, and that they are working towards being more organized and preparing more specific plans prior to negotiation.

In Argentina, a "no" answer may be seen as an intention to go back to the previous discussion. This "no" does not necessarily mean that the counterpart dismisses the possibility of making a future deal. It has been observed that both parties pursue their own interests and keep a balance between what both sides want. When one side is senses a lack of balance in the negotiation, he/she may give a "no" as an answer to create a chance to reconsider the last point discussed.

Checking information: directly or indirectly?

Ample research evidence indicates that effective information exchange promotes the development of good integrative solutions (Pruitt, 1981; Thompson, 1991; Lewicki *et al*, 1994). Some groups, such as Germans and Americans, place emphasis on direct methods of communication. Others, such as the French and Japanese, rely on indirect and complex methods (Salacuse, 1998). Eighty percent of the Argentinean executives interviewed affirmed that asking in an indirect manner is the best way to obtain information and to maintain a good relationship with the counterpart. In certain situations, to act directly could be taken as disrespectful.

There is a long-standing and strong commercial relationship with Spanish businessmen. Because of this history, they exercise a great deal of influence over the Argentineans. Just like with Spanish negotiators, a better way to approach an Argentinean negotiator is with an indirect question.

Emotionalism: high or low?

According to Salacuse (1998), Latin Americans show their emotions at the negotiation table, while Japanese and many other Asians hide their feelings. He makes the important point that individual personality plays a role here. Casse (1982) stated that Latin Americans are emotionally sensitive and easily show their feelings. The Argentinean executives are not as rational as Americans because they behave in an emotional manner. Passionate and emotional arguments in the negotiation should not be viewed as unusual situations.

On many occasions, the executives said that they showed emotions as a way to express their friendly relationship. Most of the businessmen reported being expressive and sometimes emotional with their counterparts. In this sense, they are not comfortable with a rigid and structured process. They said they observe their colleagues' reactions and determine their next move based on these observations. The way in which Argentineans persuade people is polite and respectful, taking special care not to offend or make their counterpart feel uncomfortable. In addition, they also pointed that their Brazilian colleagues are too tough and start the persuasion stage aggressively.

How to react to the counterpart's behavior

More than 75 percent of the interviewees affirmed that if the counterparts were aggressive, they would act defensively and only pursue their own interests. One of the businessmen asserted, *"If I am attacked, I attack."* In these cases, a loss of temper may be a characteristic of inexperienced negotiators. When an individual trying to conduct business with an Argentinean uses an aggressive approach, this will lead to a frustrating negotiation. In such cases, the Argentinean is usually not comfortable with the aggressive style and would probably abandon the negotiation table. Also, it will be difficult for the foreign party to reach a deal if he/she is only considering his/her own interests and appears to have no intention of pursuing a mutually successful relationship.

In Argentina, "personal relationships" tend to be long-term relationships. However, due to actual matters of planning and knowledge of political-economic events, "business relationships" tend to have short-term objectives.

- **Personal relation**: Whether the business is closed or not, the Argentinean businessman will try to maintain the level of friendship and trust. They will always express and preserve respect for the other person.

- **Business relation**: Due to the difficult task of long-term planning, it is more common to deal with short-term business objectives. Nevertheless, there exists a desire by all the executives to conduct long-term business.

According to Volkema and Chang (1998), Latin Americans prefer to do business with someone they enjoy and trust, not simply because the other party has the best product or service. The interviews revealed a clear desire for friendship and trust. This affiliation can sometimes be more important that the power of persuasion. As a clear example of the importance that Argentinean businessmen place on personal relationships, many negotiators invite their counterparts to their homes and even introduce them to their families. In this situation some businessmen admitted to having more trust in the individual counterpart than in the institutions. In some businesses, statements such as "*he will not terminate the agreement, he is my friend*" are commonly heard. This occurs especially in the Latin-American environment. On the contrary, in countries such as England, United States, France, and Germany, trust is mostly placed in the institutions.

From the '60s to the early '80s, the Argentinean government was largely controlled by the military. Due to its somewhat unstable democratic system and the frequent changes in the policies implemented by the de facto governments, a lack of trust in justice took root and corruption grew.

Therefore, some businessmen affirmed that they preferred to reach a *private* agreement between the parties. Occasionally, it is more beneficial to reach a private agreement than to win a trial in court because of the cost and time it takes to work within the Argentinean judicial system. There exists a lack of confidence in the legal system, which can at times be inefficient and slow.

Regarding a separate matter, it is important to mention that many Argentineans of Italian origins are more extroverted, expressive with body language and tend to raise their voice to defend or express certain ideas. These attributes are not necessarily wrong, but according to those interviewed, caution is advised because if the situation changes and the offence is perceived to be of a personal nature, it will certainly cause damage to the relationship between the parties.

Negotiation attitudes: "win/win or win/lose"

The win/win negotiators see deal-making as a collaborative and problem-solving process. On the other hand, win/lose negotiators see it as confrontational (Salacuse, 1998). Nearly 80 percent of the executives affirmed that if the counterpart acts in an aggressive way, they would take that same attitude. The Argentineans will probably act indirectly, trying to avoid confrontation, but they will try to continue showing their respect.
Walton and McKersie (1965) claim that the fundamental structure of a win/win negotiation situation is that it is possible for both sides to achieve their objectives. Executives identified the best business as one in which all parties are satisfied with the result of the negotiation. Emphasizing that, though it does not always occur, Argentinean negotiators take a win/win attitude. They stressed that difficulties arise from the abuse of power by many companies and from the concentration of decision-makers in certain sectors of the economy.

There exists a feeling that when dealing with international companies, the attitude is win/lose. An excellent observation from Jeswald Salacuse (1991) is that developing country officials often view their negotiations with large multinational corporations as win/lose competitions.

It used to be thought that just one party wins. For example, in the United States, there is a popular image of a used car salesman who forces the sale. That example and others like it show how parties tried to take advantage of their counterparts. However, today there exists an awareness oriented towards flexibility and cooperation between the parties.

Interests

Lax and Sebenius (1986) argued that interests include anything that the negotiator cares about and any concerns that are raised by the issues discussed. Also, they emphasized that clarifying interests could sometimes be difficult. In the interviews, businessmen asserted, *"Each party should pursue its own interests, or at least know how to identify them clearly."* Moreover, one of them stated, *"The identification of interests is not always an easy task."* They agreed on the importance of having a working knowledge and comprehension of the counterpart's interests. (Almost 60 percent of the executives agreed with this statement.) Sometimes they considered it necessary to give some concessions to maintain the other party's interest in the negotiation. It is well known that only pursuing one's own interests may lead to an unsuccessful negotiation and an unfulfilled project. Executives affirmed that it is difficult but necessary to also pursue what the counterpart needs in order to satisfy both interests. What's more, most executives agreed with Robert Axelrod's (1984:3) expression, *"We all know that people are not angels, and that they tend to look after themselves and their own first."* This is due to the fact that it is thought that each side should pursue the most successful outcome in the negotiation.

Showing the other party that it is achieving its objectives is of great importance in maintaining good relations and a state of harmony between the negotiators. One businessman said, "I pursue my own interests, but I also try to show the counterpart what he is achieving." *Trying to show what the other is winning contributes to building a good relationship with the counterpart. Furthermore, having a good relationship with the counterpart is considered very significant for Argentinean companies.*

Finally, it should be noted that businessmen expressed the need to not disregard the counterpart's interest, because if that occurs, the negotiation fails. A senior executive asserted, *"We should place ourselves in the other's shoes; we should be concerned that the other party finds satisfaction in doing business with us."*

Argentineans involve many aspects in the negotiation; they build not only a business relationship, but also a friendship. Argentina's executives said that they have started to realize the value of meeting the other side's needs, in hopes of achieving of a win-win goal and building a long-term relationship.

Form of agreement: general or specific?

The more common approach used by Argentineans executives is first, to discuss all the points and, second, to grant concessions, since they believe that knowing all about the agreement will enable them to grant some concessions to the other side. More than 70 percent agreed on reaching an agreement in this way.

Here are the reasons why they want to discuss all of the points in advance:

- There exists certain mistrust about the final agreement,
- It is better to observe everything and then follow-up with a discussion,

- The discussion of every point is not conducted in a schematic manner,
- The two sides discuss all of the points, agree on the big picture and then focus on the details.

Argentineans are not as schematic nor organized as the Germans. According to Slate Emily (1994), Germans concentrate on one task and exclude all others until the task at hand is finished. However, she argues that French businesspeople enjoy the stimulation of being involved with several projects at once, and which is a shared characteristic with Argentineans.

In the past fifteen years, it was very difficult to attend a meeting where all the objectives and issues were well defined. It was unusual to present executives with clear ideas by using videos or audio-visual presentations. However, today this is changing and is of great significance and importance to the negotiation environment.

Discussion of the majority of the points and then making concessions is the most common practice for Argentinean negotiators. The executives interviewed described the Americans as "very schematic" and said that they tend to rule the direction of the negotiation. Moreover, some executives asserted that in certain circumstances they prefer to come to an agreement focusing on each and every point, but these executives are in the minority. Their strategy depends on the necessity to solve particular issues first, so as to then define the broader issues in the negotiation.

Flexibility in the negotiation

An Argentinean works towards short-term results because society is continuously confronted with immediate problems. This generates a flexible attitude on behalf of Argentinean businessmen. Moreover, the change in political climate and the current economic and financial difficulties create obstacles to pursuing long-term objectives in the business environment. Morrison *et al* (1997) stated that in years past Argentines said that their country was *"blessed by resources but cursed by politics."* They emphasized that the land's abundant natural resources should have made it one of the world's wealthiest nations, but poor leadership kept Argentina in turmoil for decades.

Many years under a closed economy contributed to the fact that small and medium-sized companies did not consider foreign trade as a viable option. The complexities involved in foreign trade were considered far too challenging for these companies. This is one of the reasons for the scarcity of Argentinean products in certain international markets. An executive affirmed, *"Argentina is learning to do business and to have an exporting mentality. We also have a young democracy and we are just now opening ourselves up to the world."*

According to Pruitt and Rubin (1986), Fisher *et al* (1991), and Lewicki *et al* (1994), in the negotiation process both (all) sides must be firm but flexible. In the interviews, more than 85 percent of businessmen asserted that with more power, one could be less flexible. Managers stated that *"If you have more power, there is no need for flexibility."* However, more than 92 percent affirmed that inflexibility might not be advisable. It is important to be flexible when negotiating with an Argentinean manager.

One of those interviewed expressed an interesting opinion that *"in practice, flexibility occurs because of power, but it should take place because of interests."* Only 30 percent of the executives said that flexibility should take place because of interests and not power.

General aspects

The most important qualities identified by Argentinean executives for being an effective negotiator are as follows: First, to have an analytical mind and the ability to solve problems. Second, good self-control, especially when it comes to emotions. Third, the verbal ability to express ideas. Fourth, the ability to prepare and plan. Fifth, the ability to gain the respect and confidence of people one is dealing with.

In order to meet influential people, relations and favors are commonly used. It is advantageous to attend the table of negotiation by recommendation. This will help with the conversation and the process of the negotiation.

Summary and conclusion

It is important to be aware of the danger of stereotypes. Accordingly, Breslin (1989) recommends that individuals be aware of the fact that they may be guilty of stereotyping or victimized by it. However, because styles of business negotiations vary substantially around the world, it is important to take cultural differences into account when meeting clients, customers, and business partners across the international negotiation table (Graham and Cateora, 1999). In addition to cultural factors, negotiators' personalities and backgrounds also influence their behavior. In any negotiation, it is important to be sensitive to the ideals of the other culture as well as the perceptions, fears, types of behavior and circumstance of those with whom the negotiator is dealing.

Generally, research has found that Argentineans are more informal negotiators, able to keep the lines of communication open, uneasy with extended silences, and show a great deal of emotion during the negotiation. They try to build long-lasting personal relationships, but are only concerned with short-term business objectives. Finally, most Argentineans prefer to go alone to negotiations and to use persuasive tactics without accepting the first "no" reply.

Sentiments, emotions and feelings should be carefully measured at the time of negotiating with an Argentinean. Furthermore, according to Ertel (1999), negotiators in general face a problem when a relationship cannot be restored through concessions, though a setback in the negotiation should not be considered a test of the relationship.

Finally, after this extensive research, the author concludes that knowing different traditions in which people communicate and negotiate are important. However, it is also important to recognize that in the field of international negotiation people from all over the world are in some ways similar and want to feel that at least he/she will win. According to Fisher *et al* (1991), people everywhere are similar to one another. They want to be loved, care about the respect of others and do not like to feel taken advantage of.

Bibliography

Learning without thought is labor lost; thought without learning is perilous. -Confucius

Ávila, F., *Tácticas para la Negociación Internacional.* Trillas, 2000.

Axelrod, R., *The Evolution of Cooperation.* Basic Books, Inc. Publishers, 1984.

Bosworth, Micahel T., *Solution Selling.* New York: Irwin Professional Publishing, 1995.

Brandenburger, A.M. and Nalebuff, B. J., *Co-opetition.* Currency Doubleday, 1998.

Breslin, W. and Rubin. J. W., *Negotiation Theory and Practice.* Program on Negotiation Books, 1999.

Breslin, W., "Breaking Away from Subtle Biases", *Negotiation Journal* Vol.5 Number 3, pp. 219-222, USA. Plenum Publishing Corporation, 1989.

Casse, P. , *Training for Multicultural Manager: A Practical and Crosscultural Approach to the Management of People.* Washington, D.C., SIERTAR International, 1982.

Chamoun-Nicolás, H., *Desarrollo de Negocios.* Agata, 2002.

Chamoun-Nicolás, H., "Aprenda a Cerrar Buenos Tratos", *Entrepreneur*, Julio 2002.

Chamoun-Nicolás, H., "*Trato Hecho-guía para una negociación sin fallas*", KN, 2003.

Cohen, Herb., *"You Can Negotiate Anything"*, Bantam Books, 1982.

Dawson, R., *El Arte de la Negociación*. Selectron, 2001.

Ertel, D., "Turning Negotiation into a Corporate Capability". *Harvard Business Review*, pp. 55 70, May-June 1999.

Fisher, R., *Beyond Machiavelli*. Penguin Books, 1996.

Fisher, R. and Brown, S., *Getting Together. Building Relationships As We Negotiate.*, Penguin Books, 1989.

Fisher, R., Ury, W. and Patton, B. *Getting to Yes*. Penguin Books, 1991.

Foster, D.A. *International Negotiation Styles: Bargaining Across Borders: How to Negotiate Business Successfully Anywhere in the World*. Chapter.8. pp. 264-293: USA, 1992.

Graham, J.L. and Herberger, R.A.Jr., "Negotiators Abroad Don't Shoot From the Hip." *Harvard Business Review*, July-August, pp.160 168,1983.

Graham, J.L. and Adler, N.J., "Cross Cultural Interaction: The International Comparison Fallacy?", *Journal of International Business Studies 20*, pp.515-537, 1989.

Graham, J.L. and Cateora, P.R., *International Marketing*, 11th edition. Chapter 19, NY: McGraw-Hill, 1999.

Gray, J., *Men are from Mars and Women are from Venus*, Harper Collins, 1992.

Hanan, Mack. *Consultative Selling*. New York: AMACOM, 1995.

Harvard Business Review: On Negotiation and Conflict Resolution, HBSP, 2000.

Hofstede, G. , *Culture's Consequences: International Differences in Work- Related Values*. Sage Publications, 1980.

Hofstede, G., *Cultures and Organizations: Software of the Mind: Intercultural Cooperation and its Importance for Survival*. HarperCollins, 1994.

Hofstede, G., The Business of International Business is Culture, In: Jackson, T. (ed.) *Cross Cultural Management*, pp. 150-165, Butterworth Heinemann Ltd, 1995.

Hofstede, G. Levels of Culture and National Cultures in Four Dimensions, In: Hickson, D. (ed.) *Exploring Management Across the World*. Chapter 1, pp. 3-13, Penguin Group, 1997.

Karras, C., *The Negotiating Game*. Harper Business, 1992.

Lax, David A. and Sebenius, James K., *The Manager as Negotiator*. The Free Press, 1986.

Lewicki, Roy J., Saunders, David M. and Minton, John W., *Negotiation: Readings, Exercises, and Cases*, 2nd ed. Chapter 4, pp. 80-108, The McGraw Hill Companies, Inc., 1994.

Mackay, H., *Swim with the Sharks Without Being Eaten Alive*. Ballantine Books, 1988.

Miller, Robert B. and Stephen E. Heiman. *Strategic Selling*. New York: Warner Books, 1986.

Morrison, T., Conaway, W and Douress, J., *Doing Business Around The World,* Dun & Bradstreet's Guide by Prentice Hall, Inc, 1997.

Nierenberg, G. ,*The Art of Negotiating.* Barnes and Noble books, 1995.

Nierenberg, G., *The Complete Negotiator.* Barnes and Noble books, 1986.

Nierenberg, G., *The Art of Creative Thinking.* Barnes and Noble books, 1996.

Pruitt, D.G. and Rubin J.Z., *Social Conflict: Escalation, Stalemate, and Settlement.* N.Y., Random House, 1986.

Pruitt, D.G., Strategy in Negotiation In: Jossey Bass Publishers, (ed.) *International Negotiation: Analysis, Approaches, Issues.* Chapter 6, pp. 78-89. USA, Jossey Bass Inc., 1991.

Rackham, Neil. *SPIN Selling.* New York: McGraw-Hill Book Company, 1988.

Raiffa, H., *The Art and Science of Negotiation.* The Belknap Press of Harvard University Press, 2000.

Ramírez, S., *El Mexicano, Psicología de sus Motivaciones.* Grijalbo, 2002.

Salacuse, J., *The Wise Advisor,* Praeger Publishers, 2000.

Salacuse, J., *Making Global Deals: What Every Executive Should Know About Negotiating Abroad,* Times Business, 1991.

Salacuse, J., *The Global Negotiator: Making, Managing and Mending*

Deals Around the World in the 21st Century: Times Business, 2000.

Salacuse, J. W. , "Ten Ways That Culture Affects Negotiating Style: Some Survey Results". Cambridge, USA, *Negotiation Journal*, pp. 221-240, July 1998.

Savage, G., Blair, J. and Sorenson, R., *Academy of Management Executive 3*, no.1 February 1989.

Selva, Chantal., *La PNL Aplicada a la Negociación*, Granica, 1998.

Shipley Associates Proposal Guide, Shipley Associates, 2001.

Siebel, Thomas M. and Michael S. Malone. *Virtual Selling*. New York. Free Press, 1996.

Slate, E., *Tips For Negotiations in Germany and France: USA,* HR Focus, July V71 n7 pp. 18(1), 1994.

Stark, P., *Todo es Negociable*, McGraw-Hill, 1995.

Stone, D., Patton, B. and Heen. S., *Difficult Conversation*s. Penguin Books, 2000.

Susskind, L. and Field. P., *Dealing with an Angry Public. The Mutual Gains Approach to Resolving Disputes*. Free Press, 1996.

Thompson, L., "Information Exchange in Negotiation", *Journal of Experimental Social Psychology*, v27, pp. 161-179, 1991.

Ury, W., *Getting Past No*. Bantam Books, 1991.

Ury, W., *The Third Side,* Penguin Books, 2000.

Volkema, R. and Chang, S., "Negotiating in Latin America: What We Know (or Think We Know) and What We Would

Like to Know". *Latin American Business Review*, USA; The Haworth Press, Inc. Vol.1(2), pp. 3-25, 1998.

Walton, Richard E. and McKersie, Robert, B. A, *Behavioural Theory of Labour Negotiations,* USA, McGraw Hill, 1965.

Watkins, M., *Breakthrough Business Negotiations, a Toolbox for Managers.*, Jossey-Bass, 2002.

Wilson, Larry. *Stop Selling, Start Partnering.* New York. John Wiley and Sons, 1995.

Wriggins, H.W. 1976., *Up for Auction: Malta Bargains with Great Britain: The Fifty Percent Solution.* Chapter 2, pp. 208-234, Anchor Press, 1971.

Young, P., Negotiation Analysis In: Young, P. (ed.) *Negotiation Analysis,* Chapter 1, pp. 1-23, The University of Michigan Press, 1994.

Zartman, I.W., The Structure of Negotiation In: Jossey Bass Publishers (ed.) *International Negotiation: Analysis, Approaches, Issues.* Chapter 5, pp. 65-77, Jossey Bass Inc, 1991.

Ziglar, Z., *ZIG ZIGLAR'S Secrets of Closing the Sale.* Berkley Books, 1985.

Ziglar, Z., *Ziglar on Selling.* Ballantine Books, 1991.

"It is our choices Harry, that show what we truly are, far more than our abilities." -J.K. Rowling. *Harry Potter and the Chamber of Secrets*

Comments to Deal. Guidelines for a Flawless Negotiation

Your comments are valuable for the purpose of enriching the future editions of this book. Please send them through our web page and by e-mail. If you would like further information about Consulting, Seminars, Graduate courses or Workshops on Strategic Planning, Negotiations, Business Development, Strategic Selling, Proposals or Presentations send your electronic request to:

hchamoun@me.com

Or write to us in the United States:

Dr. Habib Chamoun-Nicolás
Keynegotiations
P.O. Box 6558
Kingwood, Texas 77325

About the author

Over the past 25 years, Dr. Chamoun - Nicolas has been conducting negotiation and business development activities in diversified sectors, oil and gas, petroleum, petrochemical, chemical, industrial, commercial, institutional, for the sales and marketing of services and products. Among the companies he worked for are ELF Aquitaine (Total), ICA Fluor Daniel, Brown and Root. Dr. Chamoun has trained thousands business professionals on a Business Development Approach on sales and negotiation and has conducted research on How Mexicans and other cultures Negotiate. Dr. Chamoun has designed a program to train a group of Beijing International Airport Manager for cross-cultural negotiations at the University of Houston on preparation for the 2008 Beijing Olympic Games. Dr. Chamoun has participated as a negotiation judge in May 2011 at a Chinese International Negotiation competition at Beijing University.

He is the author of many articles on negotiation and the books: "Desarrollo de Negocios", in its 3rd edition and "Trato Hecho-Guía para una Negociación sin Fallas" 2nd edition, Deal 3rd edition and Negotiate Like a Phoenician, 2008.

Dr. Habib Chamoun-Nicolas was awarded with the title of honorary professor at the Faculty of entrepreneurial specialties at the Catholic University of Santiago de Guayaquil. Dr. Chamoun also was awarded the title of negotiation visiting professor at IDE Business School in Guayaquil Ecuador. Dr. Chamoun has been appointed by the city major of his hometown in Mexico as a distinguished citizen of Nueva Rosita, Coahuila, first person that receives this award.

Dr. Chamoun has received in PARIS in 2010 the Golden Cedar Award for his book Négociez comme un Phénicien recently publish in French.

He is an adjoin business professor and member of the advisory board at St. Thomas University Cameron School of Business in Houston, Member of the Academic Senate and business professor at IMADEC University in Austria and visiting professor at the Pan European University in Slovakia.

Dr. Chamoun is also a professor of international negotiations at the Istmo University in Guatemala. The areas of interest of teaching at executive MBA programs and professional development programs are negotiation and conflict resolution, persuasion, sales and cross-cultural communications, soft-skills for entrepreneurship and project management. Dr. Chamoun has been invited as academic leader of international negotiations and relations to several Monterrey TEC campuses in Mexico, among others: Leon, Irapuato, Saltillo, Torreon, Queretaro, Sinaloa, Toluca, as well as Santo Domingo, Dominican Republic.

What are people saying about the author?

"Habib is the ideal protocol for a young energetic salesman that will not give up until he gets results. Habib makes a point to get to know his clients and their needs and provides the necessary catalyst between the client and the contractor to close the deal. I have been most impressed with Habib's love and passion for sales and his ability to interact with his clients to quickly gain their trust and confidence." -*Tom Shary,* Vice President, FLUOR DANIEL, IRVINE, CALIFORNIA

"Habib Chamoun has a rare combination of intellectual curiosity and a passion and enthusiasm for his work that generates creative ideas and the drive to implement them effectively. Dr.Chamoun has leveraged his outstanding educational background, international business experience and systematic approach to achieving results to create a business development/sales methodology that is uniquely suited for the demands of global marketplace." —*Jeff Zakaryan,* Founder and President, GLOBAL STRATEGIES EXECUTIVE COACHING, INC., DANA POINT, CALIFORNIA

"I recommend Dr. Chamoun as an outstanding example of an engineer, businessman and teacher." -*Robert S. Schechter*, PhD, Professor of Chemical and Petroleum Engineering, UNIVERSITY OF TEXAS AT AUSTIN, GETTY OIL CHAIR

"Habib is a wonderful person and I am sure he provides his students and clients sound, sincere advice. "- *Mukul Sharma. Ph.D.*, Dean of Petroleum Engineering, UNIVERSITY OF TEXAS AT AUSTIN

"I consider Habib Chamoun to be a person with high professional ethics who always exhibits very high regard for the people he is working for and working with. He is intelligent and has a good comprehension of the industries and the businesses he is serving. His strong trait is his ability to relate to business clients and quickly understands the troublesome issues that they face in a highly competitive marketplace. He possesses vision of the parameters that influence market direction and is skilled in assisting clients redirect their efforts with positive business results."-*Chick Kratzer,* President, SPECIAL TALENTS INC., HOUSTON, TEXAS

"As a past participant in Dr. Habib Chamoun's courses, I can attest that materials and concepts presented have helped me tremendously in my activities as a District Sales Manager in Mexico. Dr. Chamoun has excellent insight into the needs of the modern day sales executive and masterfully conveys the view of long-term relationship management. The Chamoun method has helped me to develop long-term customer relationships that will endure the test of time and will serve to cement mutually advantageous conditions for years to come for my Company and its customers.

Dr. Chamoun succinctly describes the sales environment and how to foster robust negotiations that not only bring results, but also customize business relationships based on the situation at hand and the needs of each party. Chamoun champions cross-cultural negotiations and the importance of knowing each party's needs and expectations. I highly recommend "DEAL" to those wanting to develop a strong sales force that can bring solutions to the table and added value instead of just focusing on methods where the price of goods sold is the only strategy to close the sale". - *Mario Perches*, District Sales Manager-Norte T-Systems International, McAllen, TEXAS

About the Collaborator

Pablo M. Linzoain is an expert in strategies for the introduction to both national and international new markets. In the last ten years, he has worked for important firms in several countries of Europe, South America and the U.S. on the planning and execution of strategies and tactics for the introduction to new markets.

As he does so, he is capitalizing on his experience in different industries, including: consumer packaged goods, manufacturing, auto parts, commodities training, insurance, film and video advertising. He currently resides in the United States, commuting between the cities of Pittsburgh and Washington, as he serves as the President of Consulting Global Business, Vice President of Marketing for Fennell Consulting Group and Commercial Director for Tyerra.

He is a graduate of the Program on Negotiation at the Law School at Harvard University in Boston and of the School of Business at the Metropolitan University of Manchester, in Manchester, England, where he obtained a double degree in the Masters of International Business Administration and International Marketing. He achieved his MBA at the Institute of Administrative Science from the Universidad Católica of Cordoba, Argentina. He also achieved the certificate *"Programme of Management Update"* from the University of California, in Berkeley. He is a graduate of the School of Economic Science of the Universidad Católica of Cordoba, Argentina, where he obtained a degree in Business Administration. He is the author of numerous articles, among them, "The Argentinean Style of Negotiation"; in addition to being a frequent collaborator of prestigious publications on international negotiations.

Get Ready to Deal

Final thoughts from the author

Selling without preparation hinders the power of negotiation. In this book you have learned how to develop your client's business and get a **great deal** every time! You found out that in order to get a **great deal** you need **preparation** — preparation to understand your client needs and wants, preparation to understand your own products and services, and preparation to understand the linkages. Most importantly, you found out how to understand your client's business goals and objectives and how you can help your client to achieve them.

As you have seen, the new sales school of thought includes everything a sales professional needs to know to be successful within the new global environment and continuum of business world changes. In addition to sales and communication skills, business development principles, strategic planning, sales methodologies, and sales tools, such as how to make a winning proposal and presentation, the global sales professional must know **how to master the art and science of negotiation with cultural awareness**.

In the past, negotiation principles and tactics were only taught to buyers, while sales strategies were taught exclusively to sellers. Thus, a natural cooperative environment was converted into a shrewd competitive ambience, just like a cockfight, where the best and toughest would last and win the competition. Building customer relations can no longer thrive in a "cockfight" atmosphere. Rather, we need to learn how to cope with one another and respect the values and principles of cultural diversity. Only then we can build business relationships based on trust that will help us grow our own business in a more sensible, flexible and culturally-diverse fashion.

Reading **Deal** you have learned:

- The main idea of success comes from developing your client's business rather than only selling your products and services.
- Negotiation is not an isolated phase in the business development process. It is an integral part of the value chain. If it is considered early on the process, it will add more value and increase the negotiation power of the parties at the negotiating table.
- We can classify our business dealings as either robust or marathon negotiations. You learned how to assess your negotiations, how to move towards robust negotiations, and how to avoid marathon negotiations.
- You can minimize the entropy in your business organization and increase the odds to WIN from Prospecting, Proposals, Presentations, Contract negotiations to reach agreement and developing long-term customer relationships.
- Culture affects negotiations. You have tools and procedures on what to do when facing a culture different from yours at the negotiation table.
- The 10 P's of the sales methodology and the 6 P's of Negotiation can help you prepare to win.

A **great deal** comes with **great preparation** and that is what this book is all about.

I would invite the readers to practice what you have learned through the journey of reading this book, and get ready to **Deal**.

Best wishes,

Habib Chamoun-Nicolás, Ph.D.

Most Recent Publications

Contributed with the following chapters of the Negotiation and Conflict Resolution books:

1. Rethinking Negotiation Teaching: Innovations for Context and Culture edited by Hamline Professor of Law James Coben, Hamline International Professor of ADR Law & Practice Giuseppe De Palo, and Christopher Honeyman 2009

Chapter: The Psychology of Giving and its effect on Negotiation" by Habib Chamoun and Randy D. Hazlett

2. Venturing Beyond the Classroom: Volume 2 in the Rethinking Negotiation Teaching Series edited by Hamline Professor of Law James Coben, Hamline International Professor of ADR Law & Practice Giuseppe De Palo, and Christopher Honeyman 2010

Chapter: Bazaar Dynamics: Teaching Integrative Negotiations in a Distributive Environment by Habib Chamoun-Nicolas, Jay Folberg and Randy D. Hazlett, 2010

Contribute also on Chapter: Should We Trust Grand Bazaar Carpet Sellers? By Jean François Roberge and Roy. J. Lewicki 2010

3. Assessing Our Students, Assessing Ourselves: Volume 3 in the Rethinking Negotiation Teaching Series edited by Noam Ebner, James Coben and Christopher Honeyman 2012

Chapter: Assessing Negotiation Competitions by Nuno Delicado, Horacio Falcao, Ellen Deason, Sharon Press, Shahla Ali, Eric Blanchot and Habib Chamoun-Nicolas, 2012

4. Educating Negotiators for a Connected World: Volume 4 in the Rethinking Negotiation Teaching Series (Coming in November 2012)

Chapter: As we see it by Bee Chen Goh, Habib Chamoun-Nicolas, Ellen Deason, Jay Folberg & Sukhsimranjit Singh

Chapter: Bringing the Street to the Classroom and the Student to the Street: Guided Forays into Street-wise Negotiations by Habib Chamoun-Nicolas, Boyd Fuller, David Benitez & Randy Hazlett

Chapter: Negotiation and Professional Boxing by Habib Chamoun-Nicolas, Randy D. Hazlett, Russell Mora, Gilberto Mendoza & Michael L. Welsh

Chapter: The Influence of Emotion in Negotiations: A Game Theory Framework Habib Chamoun & Randy Hazlett